AN ELEMENTARY

# INDIAN READER.

DESIGNED FOR THE USE OF STUDENTS IN
THE ANGLO VERNACULAR SCHOOLS
IN INDIA.

COMPILED BY

ARTHUR N. WOLLASTON, M.R.A.S.

H.M. INDIAN (HOME) SERVICE.

TRANSLATOR OF THE ANWAR-I-SUHAILI.

LONDON:

W<sup>M</sup> H. ALLEN & CO., 13, WATERLOO PLACE,

PALL MALL, S.W.

1877.

WM. H. ALLEN AND CO., PRINTERS, 13, WATERLOO PLACE,
PALL MALL, LONDON.

# PREFACE.

Of the numerous series of Readers designed for general instruction in this country, none are altogether adapted for the use of native scholars in India, to whom the idioms introduced must necessarily in many instances be to some degree, if not altogether, unintelligible. In these circumstances it has been thought expedient to compile a series of extracts, such as may with advantage be placed in the hands of young Oriental Students in the Anglo-Vernacular Schools, every passage being capable of translation into a native dialect. With the object of making the work as interesting as possible to the classes for whom it is more immediately designed, translations from Persian works of fiction have been introduced, as possessing in the estimation of Orientals a peculiar charm which can scarcely be expected to attach to extracts from English authors.

The selections are progressive, extending from short maxims of a few lines to passages of considerable length, for the most part either inculcating a sound moral, or imparting useful information: but especial care has been taken that, while instruction is primarily kept in view, amusement is by no means overlooked.

In some of the selections individual words have been omitted, or simpler expressions introduced, to remove as far as possible such peculiarities of idiom as it is the object of the present compilation to avoid: but this license has been sparingly used, and no gratuitous alterations have been made in the text of the authors from whose writings the quotations are gathered.

In addition to the primary object of the work as an Indian Reader, it is hoped that it may be suitable for general use in this country, and especially in aiding the studies of those persons who, through deficiency of early education, may wish in after years to gain a knowledge of their mother tongue. The difficulty to be surmounted in such cases is obviously the mechanical art of reading—the mind itself being more or less matured, is capable of enjoying stories of interest in place of simple elementary phrases, which, however suitable for juvenile students, are scarcely adapted for scholars of riper years.

ARTHUR N. WOLLASTON.

WESTFIELD, SURBITON,
*June*, 1877.

# CONTENTS.

|  | PAGE |
|---|---|
| Maxims | 1 and 2 |
| The Barber and the Impertinent Fellow | 3 |
| The Emperor Titus | 3 |
| A Secure Government | 3 |
| Cure for Gout | 3 |
| Anecdote of Quin the Actor | 3 |
| The Fox and the Grapes | 4 |
| The Doctor and his Patients | 4 |
| The Philosopher and the Fool | 4 |
| Anecdote of the Chief Magistrate of London | 4 |
| Maxim | 4 |
| Politeness | 5 |
| Maxim | 5 |
| The Kid and the Wolf | 5 |
| Maxim | 5 |
| Fable—The Goose and the Golden Egg | 6 |
| The Darwísh and the Thief | 6 |
| Zeno and his Rich Pupils | 6 |
| Fable—The Geese and the Cranes | 6 |
| The Little Boy and the Dead Bird | 7 |
| Maxims | 7 |
| The Quarrel between Two Gentlemen | 7 |
| The Roman General who was solicited to betray his Trust | 8 |
| Socrates and his Pupil | 8 |
| The Blind Man who went forth with a Lantern and Pitcher | 8 |
| King George I. and the Eggs | 9 |
| Anecdote of Lukmán the Sage | 9 |
| Dr. Johnson and the Widow | 9 |
| Sultan Alexander and the Madman | 10 |
| The Man with a Bad Memory | 10 |
| Chinese Maxims | 10 |
| The Earthern and Brass Pots | 10 |
| Lord Chesterfield and the Waiter | 11 |
| African Ants | 11 |
| The Poet and the Rich Man | 11 |
| The Man with Sore Eyes and the Horse Doctor | 12 |
| Fable—The Dog and the Piece of Flesh | 12 |
| The Magistrate's Mode of Detecting a Thief | 13 |

## CONTENTS.

| | PAGE |
|---|---|
| Anecdote of King Henry IV. and his Son | 13 |
| Fable—The Bald Knight | 13 |
| Anecdote of Savage | 14 |
| Knowledge | 14 |
| Fable—The Crow and the Pitcher | 15 |
| Anecdote of Walter Scott and the Boy with a Button | 15 |
| Fable—The Lion and the Bulls | 15 |
| The Monkeys and their Dead Comrade | 16 |
| Fable—The Hare and the Bramble | 17 |
| Anecdote of Hátim Táí | 17 |
| The Roman Citadel saved by Geese | 18 |
| Sir Peter Lely and the Rich Merchant | 18 |
| The Woman and her Lover | 19 |
| Prince Henry and the Judge | 19 |
| Fable—The Skylark | 20 |
| Hátim Táí and the Ambassador | 20 |
| Sir Richard Steele and the Workman | 20 |
| The Lawyer and his Ugly Daughter | 21 |
| Canute's Reproof to his Courtiers | 21 |
| Fable—The Fox and the Goat | 22 |
| The Slave and his Master | 22 |
| Michael Angelo and the Statue | 23 |
| A Piece of Chalk | 23 |
| The Parrot which spoke Persian | 24 |
| Fable—The Old Hound | 24 |
| Anecdote of Alfred the Great | 25 |
| The Miser and his Friend | 25 |
| Anecdote of the Emperor Joseph II. | 26 |
| Fable—The Peacock and Juno | 26 |
| A Raven that Entertained the Chickens | 27 |
| Sir William Napier and the Little Girl | 28 |
| The King of Persia and the Boy | 28 |
| Fable—The Eagle and the Fox | 29 |
| Birds | 30 |
| The Trumpeter and the Hyena | 31 |
| The Courtier and the Thieves | 31 |
| Fable—The Fox and the Stork | 32 |
| King Charles II. and the Suppliant for Office | 32 |
| Fable—The Lion and the Mouse | 33 |
| The Debtor and his Creditors | 34 |
| Sir John Jervis and the Decoy Vessels | 34 |
| Bear Catching in Russia | 35 |
| Anecdote of Dean Swift and the Servant | 35 |
| Nature | 36 |
| Anecdote of a Dog | 37 |
| The Judge's Mode of Detecting Dishonesty | 37 |

## CONTENTS.

|  | PAGE |
|---|---|
| Anecdote of St. Anthony | 38 |
| Anecdote of an Elephant | 39 |
| Napoleon and the Arab | 40 |
| Fable—The Hares and the Frogs | 40 |
| Abraham and the Traveller | 41 |
| King Richard I. and Blondel | 42 |
| The King who fancied his Minister was guilty of Exaggeration | 43 |
| Sagacity of a Fox | 43 |
| Anecdote of Dr. Paley | 44 |
| Fable—The Shepherd and his Dog | 45 |
| Truth | 46 |
| Fable—The Nightingale and the Hawk | 46 |
| Anecdote of a Sick Elephant | 47 |
| Lines to a Newfoundland Dog | 48 |
| The Wise Man and the Chemist | 48 |
| The Two Goldfinches | 49 |
| The Covetous Man and his Axe | 50 |
| The Dispute between the Hunting Hawk and the Domestic Fowl | 51 |
| The Arab and his Horse | 52 |
| The Old Man and his Ass | 53 |
| Fable—The Kite and the Pigeons | 54 |
| The Merchant and the Bad tempered Horse | 55 |
| Anecdote of Sultan Mahmoud | 56 |
| The Deaf Man, the Blind Man, and the Whip | 57 |
| Sagacity of a Dog | 59 |
| Robinson Crusoe | 60 |
| Anecdote of an Eagle | 62 |
| The Porcupine, Chameleon, and Owl | 63 |
| The Judge and the Merchant's Property | 64 |
| The Jackal who was elected King of the Animals | 65 |
| Asem the Recluse | 66 |
| Fable—The Cock and the Fox | 67 |
| Adventure with an Alligator | 68 |
| Alexander Severus and his Soldiers | 70 |
| Fable—The Fox and the Wolf | 71 |
| Anecdote of Queen Margaret | 72 |
| Fable—The Wolf and the Mastiff | 73 |
| A Raven that went to a Fair | 74 |
| Fable—The Foolish Young Cock | 76 |
| Anecdote of a Cat | 77 |
| The Horatii and Curiatii | 79 |
| The Tame Bear | 80 |
| The Flea, the Grasshopper, and the Cricket | 82 |

## CONTENTS.

|  | PAGE |
|---|---|
| The Wrestler and his Pupil | 83 |
| The Result of Avarice | 85 |
| Invasion of England by the Danes | 86 |
| Anecdote of a Crossing-Sweeper | 88 |
| The Nobleman and the Serpent | 89 |
| The Two Shepherds | 91 |
| Robinson Crusoe | 92 |
| The Jackal and the Camel | 94 |
| Ulysses and his Dog | 95 |
| Fable—The Lark and her Young Ones | 96 |
| The Poor Cobbler and the Fairies | 97 |
| Anecdote of M. Berryer | 99 |
| Education in India | 100 |
| Livingstone and the Lion | 101 |
| The Goldsmith and the Soldier | 103 |
| Fable—The Town Mouse and the Country Mouse | 105 |
| The Bald Eagle | 107 |
| The Dog and the Crane | 109 |
| The Charge of the Light Brigade | 111 |
| The Monkey and the Child | 113 |
| The Ant | 116 |
| Death of the Son of King Henry I. | 116 |
| African Monkeys on March | 119 |
| Conversation of the Vultures | 121 |
| The Lion and the Jackals | 124 |
| Time | 126 |
| Buckwheat: A Legend | 126 |
| Anecdote of Baron Cuvier | 128 |
| The Thieves and the Peasant | 131 |
| The Parrot and the King | 133 |
| Creation | 135 |
| The Boar and the Two Lions | 135 |
| The Three Fish | 138 |
| Murad the Unlucky | 141 |
| The Choice of Hercules | 143 |
| The Vanity of Riches | 146 |
| The Spider | 149 |
| Scenes in India | 151 |
| Advice to Young Men | 154 |
| The Chamois, and Chamois Hunting | 156 |
| Valour | 160 |
| A Boar Hunt | 164 |
| The Burial of Sir John Moore | 168 |
| The Little Daisy | 169 |
| The Blind Man and the Deaf Man | 173 |
| A Psalm of Life | 181 |

# INDIAN READER.

### MAXIM.

Nature has given us two ears and only one mouth, in order that we may listen much and speak little.—ANON.

### MAXIM.

The good things which belong to prosperity are to be desired; but the good things which belong to adversity are to be admired.—SENECA.

### MAXIM.

In taking revenge a man is but even with his enemy, but in passing it over he is superior.—BACON.

### MAXIM.

To show mercy to the wicked is injustice to the good, and to pardon oppressors is to wrong the oppressed.—GULISTAN.

#### MAXIM.

Envy is a fire which, when it flares up, burns everything whether moist or dry; and excessive jealousy so influences a man that he cannot see even what is for his own good.—FABLES OF BIDPAI.

#### MAXIM.

Our thoughts are our own whilst we keep them in our hearts, but when once we let them escape they are in the power of another, who may make use of them to our injury.—ANON.

#### MAXIM.

Speak in such wise between two enemies that, if they become friends, thou mayst not be ashamed.—GULISTAN.

#### MAXIM.

Reading furnishes the mind only with materials of knowledge; it is thinking makes what we read ours.—LOCKE.

#### MAXIM.

Two persons undergo useless trouble, and exert themselves to no purpose. One, he who amasses riches and does not enjoy them; the other, he who acquires knowledge and does not act according to it.—GULISTAN.

#### MAXIM.

If we saw ourselves in the light in which others see us, or in which they would see us if they knew all, a reformation would generally be unavoidable. We could not otherwise endure the sight.—ADAM SMITH.

### THE BARBER AND THE IMPERTINENT FELLOW.

A conceited impertinent fellow once said to a barber, "Did you ever shave a monkey?" "Why, no sir," replied the man, "never; but if you will please to sit down I will try."—ANON.

### THE EMPEROR TITUS.

The Emperor Titus said, "If anyone speaks ill of me, I must take care not to punish him; if he has spoken through carelessness, I must despise him; if through folly, I must pity him; if it be an injury, I must pardon him."—ANON.

### A SECURE GOVERNMENT.

A philosopher of Greece being asked under what government men could live with the greatest security, and least danger, answered, "Under that where virtue finds many friends, and where vice finds few partisans, or has none at all."—ANON.

### CURE FOR GOUT.

Abernethy, the celebrated surgeon, was once asked by a rich, luxurious patient, what was the best cure for gout. "Live upon sixpence a day, and earn it!" was the answer.—ANON.

### ANECDOTE OF QUIN THE ACTOR.

When Quin, the actor, was one day lamenting his growing old, a pert young fellow asked him what he would give to be as young as he. "I would be content," replied Quin, "to be as foolish."—ANON.

### FABLE: THE FOX AND THE GRAPES.

A fox, very hungry, chanced to come into a vineyard, where there hung branches of charming ripe grapes, but nailed up so high, that he leaped till he quite tired himself, without being able to reach one of them. At last, "Let who will take them," says he, "they are but green and sour; so I will let them alone."—Æsop's Fables.

### THE DOCTOR AND HIS PATIENTS.

A doctor whenever he went into a burying-ground used to pull his mantle across his face: persons enquired of him the reason of such a proceeding: he replied, "I am ashamed on account of the men in this place of burial, since they died owing to my medicine."—Persian Tales.

### THE PHILOSOPHER AND THE FOOL.

An ignorant person one day seeing a man of learning enjoying the pleasures of the table, said, "So, sir, philosophers I see can indulge in delicacies." "Why not?" replied the other, "do you think good things were intended merely for fools?"—Anon.

### ANECDOTE OF THE CHIEF MAGISTRATE OF LONDON.

A story is told of a certain chief magistrate of London, who, hearing that a person of his acquaintance had been attacked twice with fever, and died in consequence, enquired if he died on the first or second occasion.—Anon.

### MAXIM.

There is certainly no greater happiness than to be able to look back on a life usefully and virtuously employed, to trace our own progress in existence by such tokens as excite neither shame nor sorrow.—JOHNSON.

### POLITENESS.

An officer in battle happening to stoop his head, a cannon-ball passed completely over it, and took off the head of a soldier who stood behind him. "You see," said the officer, "that a man never loses by politeness."—ANON.

### MAXIM.

The society of the ignorant and base must be avoided, and the service of the wise and good must be embraced; for companionship with the low and mean is like nourishing a viper; the more a snake-catcher may foster it, the more grief will he experience, and ultimately it will give him a taste of poison from its fangs; whereas the service of the wise and good is like a perfumer's casket, since, though none of the contents thereof may be poured upon a person, yet the odours of its scents will perfume the nostrils."—FABLES OF BIDPAI.

### FABLE—THE KID AND THE WOLF.

A kid, being mounted upon the roof of a shed, and seeing a wolf below, loaded him with all manner of reproaches: upon which, the wolf, looking up, replied, "Do not value yourself, vain creature, upon thinking you mortify me, for I look upon this ill language, as not coming from you, but from the place which protects you."—ÆSOP'S FABLES.

### MAXIM.

Nobody knows the strength of his mind, and the force of steady and regular application, until he has tried. This is certain, he that sets out upon weak legs will not only go further, but grow stronger too, than one with a vigorous constitution and firm limbs, who only sits still.—LOCKE.

### FABLE—THE GOOSE AND THE GOLDEN EGG.

A certain man had a goose which laid him a golden egg every day. But not contented with this, which rather increased than abated his avarice, he was resolved to kill the goose, so that he might come to the inexhaustible treasure, which he fancied she had within her. He did so, and to his great sorrow and disappointment found nothing.—ÆSOP'S FABLES.

### THE DARWISH* AND THE THIEF.

A certain person stole a Darwish's turban and fled. The holy man went to the burying-ground and sat there; men said to him, "That individual carried your turban towards a certain garden, why do you remain amongst the tombs?" He replied, "He nevertheless will come here; for this reason I am awaiting his arrival."—PERSIAN TALES.

### ZENO AND HIS RICH PUPILS.

Zeno, the philosopher, having remonstrated with certain of his pupils for their extravagance, they excused themselves by saying that they were rich enough to indulge in prodigality. "Would you," said he, "excuse a cook that should over-salt his meat because he had a superabundance of salt?"—ANON.

### FABLE—THE GEESE AND THE CRANES.

A flock of geese and a parcel of cranes used to feed together in a corn-field. At last, the owner of the corn,

---

* A holy man.

with his servants, coming upon them of a sudden, surprised them in the very act; and the geese being heavy, fat, full-bodied creatures, were most of them sufferers; but the cranes being thin and light, easily flew away.—ÆSOP'S FABLES.

### THE LITTLE BOY AND THE DEAD BIRD.

A gentleman, riding with his family in the country, saw a very beautiful bird. His little son about four years old, watched it with great interest. The father, thinking it would give him still more pleasure to examine its plumage, thoughtlessly raised his gun and shot it. The little boy burst into tears as his father put the dead bird into his hands, and exclaimed, "Father, that bird will never sing again!" The parent said sometime afterwards, "I can never shoot another bird!"—ANON.

### MAXIMS.

Confide not to a friend every secret that thou possessest, for it may happen that at some time he may become an enemy; and do not inflict on an enemy all the injury that is in thy power, perchance he may some day become a friend; and tell not to any person the secret which thou wouldst have hidden, even though he be a sincere friend, for that friend has other friends also.—GULISTAN.

### THE QUARREL BETWEEN TWO GENTLEMEN.

Two gentlemen having a difference, one went to the other's door early in the morning, and wrote "Scoundrel" upon it. The other called upon his neighbour, and was answered by a servant that his master was not at home, but if he had anything to say he might leave the message. "No, no," said the visitor, "I have nothing of importance to say, I only wished to return your master's visit, as he left his name at my door in the morning."—ANON.

### THE ROMAN GENERAL WHO WAS SOLICITED TO BETRAY HIS TRUST.

When a Roman general, sitting at supper with a plate of turnips before him, was solicited by large presents to betray his trust, he asked the messengers whether he that could sup on turnips was a man likely to sell his own country. Upon him who has reduced his senses to obedience, temptation has lost its power; he is able to attend impartially to virtue, and execute her commands without hesitation.—JOHNSON.

### SOCRATES AND HIS PUPIL.

A young man who was a great talker, was sent by his parents to Socrates to learn oratory. On being presented to Socrates, the lad spoke so much that Socrates was out of patience. When the bargain came to be struck, Socrates asked him double the price.—" Why charge me double?" said the young fellow, " Because," said the orator, " I must teach you two sciences; the one to hold your tongue, and the other how to speak."—ANON.

### THE BLIND MAN WHO WENT FORTH WITH A LANTERN AND PITCHER.

A blind man one dark evening took a lantern in his hand, and a pitcher on his shoulders, and went to the market. A person enquired of him, " O foolish fellow! since day and night are the same to your eyes, of what advantage is a lantern to you.?" The blind man smiled and said, " This lantern is not on my own account, but rather that the evening being dark you may not break my pitcher.—PERSIAN TALES.

### KING GEORGE I. AND THE EGGS.

King George I. on a journey to Hanover, stopped at a village in Holland, and while horses were getting ready for him, he asked for two or three eggs, which were brought him, and charged a hundred florins. "How is this?" said the King, "eggs must be very scarce here." "Pardon me," said the host, "eggs are plentiful enough, but Kings are scarce."—ANON.

### ANECDOTE OF LUKMAN THE SAGE.

They said to Lukmān the Sage, "Of whom didst thou learn manners?" "Of all the ill-mannered," he replied, "for anything on their part which was disapproved in my sight I avoided."

> People utter not a word, even in jest,
> But what sensible men learn a lesson therefrom;
> But if to a fool a hundred chapters on wisdom
> People read, they would be as jesting to his ear.—
> GULISTAN.

### DR. JOHNSON AND THE WIDOW.

When Dr. Johnson asked the Widow Porter to be his wife, he told her candidly that he had no money, and that his uncle had been hanged. The widow replied that she cared nothing for his parentage; that she had no money herself; and that, though she had no relation hanged, she had fifty who deserved hanging.—ANON.

### SULTAN ALEXANDER AND THE MADMAN.

Sultán Alexander the Great one day passed by a man who was mad, and said, "O friend! ask somewhat of me." He replied, "The flies are annoying me, bid them cease." The King rejoined, "O mad fellow! demand something which is in my power." The man said, "Seeing that not even a fly is under your control, what can I ask."—PERSIAN TALES.

### THE MAN WITH A BAD MEMORY.

A gentleman had so bad a memory, and so circumscribed that he scarce knew what he read. A friend, aware of this, lent him the same book to read seven times over; being asked afterwards how he liked it, he replied, "I think it is an admirable production, but the author sometimes repeats the same things."—ANON.

### CHINESE MAXIMS.

Let every man sweep the snow away from his own door, and not busy himself about the frost on his neighbour's tiles.

Great wealth comes by destiny; moderate wealth by industry.

The ripest fruit will not fall into your mouth.

The pleasure of doing good is the only one that does not wear out.

Dig a well before you are thirsty.

Water does not remain in the mountains, nor vengeance in a great mind.—ANON.

### FABLE.—THE EARTHEN AND BRASS POTS.

An Earthen Pot, and one of Brass, standing together

upon the river's brink, were both carried away by the flowing in of the tide. The Earthen Pot shewed some uneasiness, as fearing he should be broken; but his companion of Brass bid him be under no apprehension, for that he would take care of him. "O," replies the other, "keep as far off as ever you can I entreat you! it is you I am most afraid of; for, whether the stream washes you against me, or me against you, I am sure to be the sufferer! and therefore I beg of you do not let us come near one another."—Æsop's Fables.

### Lord Chesterfield and the Waiter.

Lord Chesterfield one day, at an inn where he dined, complained very much that the plates and dishes were very dirty. The waiter, with a degree of pertness, observed, "It is said that one must eat a peck of dirt before he dies." "That may be true," said Chesterfield, "but no one is obliged to eat it all at one meal."—Anon.

### African Ants.

African ants sometimes set forward in such multitudes that the whole earth seems to be in motion. A body of them was once seen to attack and cover an elephant, quietly feeding in a pasture. In eight hours nothing was to be seen but the skeleton of that enormous animal completely picked. The business was done, and the enemy marched on after fresh prey. Such power have the smallest creatures acting in concert.—Anon.

### The Poet and the Rich Man.

A certain poet went to the presence of a rich man, and sang his praises: the grandee was delighted and said, "I have no money with me, but if you call to-morrow I will give you some corn." The poet returned to his own home, and next day at dawn repaired to the rich man, who enquired, "why have you come?" "Yesterday" said the man "you promised to give me some corn, for this reason am I here." The grandee smiled, and said " you are a wonderfully foolish fellow; you pleased me with your words, and I, too, rendered you happy, now why should I give you any corn?" The poet was ashamed, and retired.—PERSIAN TALES.

### THE MAN WITH SORE EYES AND THE HORSE-DOCTOR.

A man got sore eyes. He went to a horse-doctor, and said, "Treat me." The veterinary surgeon applied to the eyes a little of what he was in the habit of putting into the eyes of quadrupeds, and the man became blind. They carried the case before the judge, who said, "No damages are to be recovered from him; if this fellow had not been an ass, he would not have gone to a farrier." The object of this story is, that thou mayest know, that he who entrusts an important matter to an inexperienced person, will suffer regret, and the wise will impute weakness of intellect to him.—GULISTAN.

### FABLE—THE DOG AND THE PIECE OF FLESH.

A dog, crossing a rivulet, with a piece of flesh in his mouth, saw his own shadow represented in the clear mirror of the limpid stream; and believing it to be another dog, who was carrying also a piece of flesh, he could not forbear catching at it; but was so far from getting anything by his greedy design, that he dropt the piece he had in his mouth, which immediately sunk to the bottom, and was irrecoverably lost.—ÆSOP'S FABLES.

### THE MAGISTRATE'S MODE OF DETECTING A THIEF.

A certain person lost a purse of money in a house, and informed the magistrate thereof. The latter summoned all the inmates of the place, and taking several pieces of wood, all of an equal length, gave one to each of them, and said, "The piece of wood in the hands of the thief will prove to be an inch longer than that of the others." After they had all been dismissed, the individual who had stolen the money became alarmed, and cut off an inch from his stick. Next day when the judge summoned all of them, and examined the pieces of wood, he at once discovered who was the thief, and punished him accordingly.—PERSIAN TALES.

### ANECDOTE OF KING HENRY IV AND HIS SON.

The last years of the life of Henry IV. of England were much enfeebled by ill health: he became childishly anxious about his crown, placing it always on his pillow, lest it should be seized before he was dead. One day, the prince being in his father's chamber, and not perceiving him to breathe, believed him dead, and removed the crown from the pillow, for which the king on awakening, severely reproved him, at the same time reminding him that neither he nor his father had any good right to it.

"My Lord," replied Henry, "it is my intention to hold and defend it by my sword as you have done."

STORIES FROM ENGLISH HISTORY (HALL.)

### FABLE—THE BALD KNIGHT.

A certain knight growing old, his hair fell off, and he became bald: to hide which imperfection, he wore a wig. But as he was riding out with some others hunting, a sudden gust of wind blew off the wig, and exposed his bald pate. The company could not forbear laughing at the accident, and he himself laughed as loud as anybody, saying, "How was it to be expected that I should keep strange hair upon my head, when my own would not stay there?"—ÆSOP'S FABLES.

### ANECDOTE OF SAVAGE.

During a considerable part of the time in which Savage was employed upon his tragedy of "Sir Thomas Overbury," he was without lodging, and often without meat; nor had he any other conveniences for study allowed him than the fields or the streets; there he used to walk and form his speeches, and afterwards step into a shop, beg the use of the pen and ink for a few moments, and write down what he had composed upon paper which he had picked up by accident.—ANON.

### KNOWLEDGE.

A philosopher was advising his sons, and saying, "My dear boys! acquire knowledge; for no reliance should be placed on the possessions and wealth of the world, since silver and gold on a journey (like life's) are an abiding source of affliction; for a thief may carry off all at a swoop, or the owner by degrees spend all; but knowledge is a never-failing fount, and an everlasting treasure. If a man possessed of knowledge fall from riches (into poverty), it is of no consequence, for knowledge is wealth in itself; wherever he goes he meets with esteem, and sits in the seat of honour; whereas the man without knowledge picks up scraps of food, and experiences hardship."—GULISTAN.

### FABLE—THE CROW AND THE PITCHER.

A crow, ready to die with thirst, flew with joy to a pitcher, which he beheld at some distance. When he came, he found water in it indeed, but so near the bottom, that with all his stooping and straining he was not able to reach it. Then he endeavoured to overturn the pitcher, that so at least he might be able to get a little of it. But his strength was not sufficient for this. At last, seeing some pebbles lie near the place, he cast them one by one into the pitcher, and thus, by degrees, raised the water up to the very brim, and satisfied his thirst.—ÆSOP'S FABLES.

### ANECDOTE OF WALTER SCOTT AND THE BOY WITH A BUTTON.

There was a boy in my class, who always stood at the top, and with all my efforts I could not get above him. Days passed, but still he kept his place, do what I would; but at last I noticed that whenever a question was asked him he fumbled with his fingers at a particular button on his waistcoat. In an evil moment I removed it with a knife. When the boy was again questioned, his fingers sought the button in vain; in his distress he looked down for it, but it was not to be seen, and as he stood confounded I took his place, nor did he ever guess who was the author of his wrong. Often in after-life has the sight of him smote me as I passed by him, and I resolved to make him some reparation, but it always ended in good resolutions.—WALTER SCOTT.

### FABLE—THE LION AND THE BULLS.

Four bulls, which had entered into a very strict friendship, kept always near one another, and fed together. The lion often saw them, and as often had a mind to make

one of them his prey; but though he could easily have subdued any of them singly, yet he was afraid to attack the whole alliance, as knowing they would have been too hard for him, and therefore contented himself for the present with keeping at a distance. At last, perceiving no attempt was to be made upon them as long as this combination held, he took occasion, by whispers and hints, to ferment jealousies and raise divisions among them. This stratagem succeeded so well, that the bulls grew cold and reserved towards one another, which soon after ripened into a downright hatred and aversion, and, at last, ended in a total separation. The lion had now obtained his ends; and, impossible as it was for him to hurt them while they were united, he found no difficulty, now they were parted, to seize and devour every bull of them, one after another.
—ÆSOP'S FABLES.

### ANECDOTE—THE MONKEYS AND THEIR DEAD COMRADE.

On a shooting expedition one of the party killed a female monkey under a banian tree, and carried it to his tent, which was soon surrounded by forty or fifty of the tribe, who made a great noise, and seemed disposed to attack the aggressor. They retreated when he presented his gun, the dreadful effect of which they had witnessed, and appeared perfectly to understand. The head of the troop, however, stood his ground, chattering furiously. The sportsman, who perhaps felt some little degree of compunction at having killed one of the family, did not like to fire at the creature, and nothing short of firing at him would suffice to drive him off. At length the ape came to the door of the tent, and finding threats of no avail began a lamentable moaning, and by the most expressive gestures seemed to beg for the dead body. It was given him; he took it sorrowfully in

his arms, and bore it away to his expecting companions.—
CASSELL's NATURAL HISTORY.

### FABLE—THE HARE AND THE BRAMBLE.

A hare, closely pursued, thought it prudent and meet,
To a bramble for refuge awhile to retreat;
He enter'd the covert, but, entering, found
That briers and thorns did on all sides abound;
And that, though he was safe, yet he never could stir,
But his sides they would wound, or would tear off his fur;
He shrugg'd up his shoulders, but would not complain;
"To repine at small evils," quoth Puss, "is in vain;
That no bliss can be perfect I very well know;
But from the same source good and evil both flow:
And full sorely my skin though these briers may rend,
Yet they keep off the dogs, and my life will defend:
For the sake of the good, then, let evil be borne;
For each sweet has its bitter, each bramble its thorn."—
NORTHCOTE's FABLES.

### ANECDOTE OF HATIM TAI

They said to Hātim Tā,ī, "Hast thou seen a person in the world more magnanimous than thyself?" He replied, "Yes, one day I had sacrificed forty camels, and invited some Arabian chieftains; all of a sudden I went through necessity to a retired part of the desert, and saw a woodman with a bundle of sticks gathered together; I said, "Why dost thou not go to Hātim's entertainment? for a vast concourse of people have assembled at his board." He replied,

"Whoso eateth the bread of his own labour
"Will be under no obligation to Hātim of Tāyī."

I considered him superior to myself in magnanimity and generosity.—GULISTAN.

### THE ROMAN CITADEL SAVED BY GEESE.

The Gauls observed the footsteps on the side of the hill, and an attempt was made by Brennus to scale the side as the Roman had done. Accordingly a few of the most courageous ascended to the base of the wall undiscovered; but the well-known watchfulness of some geese, that belonged to the temple of Juno (to whom they were sacred), saved the capitol. The poor birds, made more watchful by their hunger, awakened the men who lay near. A Roman hastened to the wall, and found that two Gauls had mounted it. They were both struck and hurled down the rampart. The sentinel was punished, and the geese ever after were held in due honour.—STORIES FROM THE HISTORY OF ROME.

### SIR PETER LELY AND THE RICH MERCHANT.

Sir Peter Lely had agreed for the price of a portrait he was to draw for a rich London merchant, who was not indebted to nature either for shape or face. The picture being finished, the merchant endeavoured to lower the price, saying, that if he did not purchase the picture it would remain on the painter's hands. "That is a mistake," said Sir Peter, "for I can sell it for double the price I demand." "How can that be?" enquired the merchant, "for it is like no one but myself." "True," replied the painter, "but I will draw a tail to it, and then it will be a capital monkey." The merchant at once paid the money demanded, and carried off the picture.—ANON.

### THE WOMAN AND HER LOVER.

A certain woman was walking along, and a man seeing her, proceeded after her. The woman enquired, "Why do you follow me?" He replied, "Because I am in love with you." She rejoined, "Why should you be in love with me, my sister is more handsome, and she is coming behind me; go and make love to her." The man departed thence, and seeing that the damsel was ugly became much displeased, and again approached the former woman, exclaiming, "Why did you speak falsely?" she replied, "you too did not adhere to the truth, since if you were in love with me why did you turn away to another person?"—PERSIAN TALES.

### PRINCE HENRY AND THE JUDGE.

One of the favourites of Prince Henry, eldest son of King Henry IV. of England being arraigned for felony before Chief Justice Gascoigne, the prince resolved to be present at the trial, with the design to overawe the judge. But his presence not preventing the criminal's condemnation, he was so enraged that he struck the judge on the face. The chief justice, considering the consequences of such an act, instantly commanded him to be arrested on the spot, and conveyed to prison, The royal offender, instead of resisting, as might have been expected, permitted himself to be taken away. Hearing this, the king was so much gratified that he exclaimed, "Happy the king who has so faithful a magistrate, and still more happy the parent who has a son willing to submit to such a chastisement."—STORIES FROM ENGLISH HISTORY (HALL).

### FABLE—THE SKYLARK.

When day's bright banner, first unfurl'd,
From darkness frees the shrouded world,
The Skylark, singing as he soars,
On the fresh air his carol pours;
But though to heaven he wings his flight,
As if he loved those realms of light,
He still returns with weary wing,
On earth to end his wandering.—

NORTHCOTE'S FABLES.

### HATIM TAI AND THE AMBASSADOR.

The Greek Emperor sent an ambassador to Yaman to demand on the part of his master a favourite horse which Hātim Tāī possessed. The generous Arab had received no intimation either of the embassy or of its object: when the ambassador therefore arrived, Hātim was quite unprepared for his reception. In order to prepare a suitable entertainment for his illustrious guest and his attendants, he had no other resource than to cause his favourite horse to be killed and roasted on the occasion. This was accordingly done: and after the feast the ambassador stated his master wish. "It is too late," replied Hātim, "the horse has been killed for our repast. When you arrived, I knew not the object of your journey, and I had no other food to offer you."—D'HERBELOT.

### SIR RICHARD STEELE AND THE WORKMAN.

When Sir Richard Steele was fitting up his great room for public orations, he happened at one time to be in arrear in paying his workmen; coming one day to see how the work was progressing, he ordered one of them to get into the reading-desk and make a speech with a view of testing the capabilities of the room. The man was at a loss what to say, not being an orator. "Oh," said Sir Richard, "no matter for that, speak anything that enters your mind." " Why Sir," exclaimed the workman, " we have been working for you these six weeks, and cannot get any money: pray Sir, when do you design to pay us?" "Stop, man!" said Sir Richard, somewhat embarrassed, "I have heard enough. I cannot but own you speak very distinctly, though I must admit I do not admire your choice of a subject."—ANON,

### THE LAWYER AND HIS UGLY DAUGHTER.

A lawyer had a daughter—ugly in the extreme—arrived at the verge of maturity, and, despite a dowry and much wealth, no one showed an inclination to marry her.
Hideous would be the stuff of gold tissue, and the coloured
  silk brocade.
Which were on an uncomely bride!
In brief, under pressure of necessity, they married her to a blind man. They tell that at that time a physician arrived from Ceylon, who used to restore sight to the eyes of the blind. They said to the lawyer, "Why dost thou not have thy son-in-law treated?" He replied, "I fear he would recover his sight and divorce my daughter."

The husband of an ugly woman is best blind.—GULISTAN.

### CANUTE'S REPROOF TO HIS COURTIERS.

Canute's reproof to his courtiers is well known. These unworthy flatterers declaring him the commander of the ocean itself, he ordered the chair of his dignity to be placed on the sea-beach, and thus addressed the tide that was rolling to shore:—"Keep back, thou proud ocean! the island on which I sit is mine: thou art a part of my dominions, and I forbid thee to ascend my coasts, or to presume to wet the borders of my robes." That this mandate was disregarded will be obvious, and Canute availed himself of the occasion to impress on the mind of his courtiers this sublime truth, "God only is the Great Supreme! let Him only have the name of Majesty whose everlasting laws the heavens, earth and sea with all their hosts obey!"—STORIES FROM ENGLISH HISTORY (HALL.)

### FABLE—THE FOX AND THE GOAT.

A fox having tumbled by chance into a well, had been casting about for a long while to no purpose, how he should get out again, when at last a goat came to the place and wanting to drink asked Reynard whether the water was good. "Good!" says he, "ay, so sweet, that I am afraid I have surfeited myself, I have drunk so abundantly." The goat, upon this, without any more ado, leapt in; and the fox, taking the advantage of his horns, by the assistance of them, as nimbly leapt out, leaving the poor goat at the bottom of the well, to shift for himself.—ÆSOP's FABLES.

### THE SLAVE AND HIS MASTER.

A slave fled from his master. After several days, the latter, on visiting another city, saw him there and seized him, saying, "Why did you run away?" The slave laid his hand on his master's sleeve and exclaimed, "You are my servant, and have robbed me of much money, and fled: now I have found you I will punish you." In short, both of them repaired to the judge and demanded justice. The judge ordered them both to put their heads out of window. When they had done so, he commanded an executioner to cut off the slave's head. When the slave heard this order he at once drew in his head. while his master did not move. The judge punished the miscreant and delivered him over to his owner.—PERSIAN TALES.

### MICHAEL ANGELO AND THE STATUE.

A friend called on Michael Angelo, who was finishing a statue. Some time afterwards he called again. The sculptor was still at his work. His friend, looking at the figure, exclaimed, "You have been idle since I saw you last." "By no means," replied the sculptor; "I have retouched this part and polished that; I have softened this feature and brought out this muscle; I have given more expression to this lip, and more energy to this limb." "Well, well!" said his friend, "but all these are trifles." "It may be so," replied Angelo, "but recollect that trifles make perfection, and that perfection is no trifle."—ANON.

### A PIECE OF CHALK.

If a small piece of chalk is moistened and rubbed on a piece of glass, and placed under a powerful microscope, myriads of very small things are seen. Some are fragments of larger things, but the greater part consist of the minute skeletons and shells of little tiny creatures. Much of the chalk consists, also, of round grains, which when broken are found to contain other grains arranged in circles round a centre. These are all remnants of very small creatures, which were once alive. So small are they, that 10,000 of them placed in a row would not make up an inch in length. The shapes of the little shells are very pretty, and they are beautifully marked with dots and lines, so as to form very interesting objects under a good microscope.—WORLD OF WONDERS.

### THE PARROT WHICH SPOKE PERSIAN.

A certain person reared a parrot, and taught it the Persian language, so that to every question which might be asked it should answer, "What doubt?" One day the man took it to the bāzār with the object of selling it, and demanded a large sum as the price thereof. A person who had happened to see the bird enquired of it, "Are you worth so much money?" It replied, "What doubt?" The man was delighted, and purchasing the parrot took it to his own home. To every word he uttered the creature gave the same answer. Ashamed and with a heart filled with regret the fellow exclaimed, "What a fool I was to buy this parrot!" "What doubt?" was the immediate rejoinder. Smiling at the drollness of the incident, the man gave the bird its freedom.—PERSIAN TALES.

### FABLE—THE OLD HOUND.

An old hound, who had been an excellent good one in his time, and given his master great sport and satisfaction in many a chase, at last by the effect of years became feeble and unserviceable. However, being in the field one day when the stag was almost run down, he happened to be the first that came in with him, and seized him by one of his haunches; but his decayed and broken teeth not being able to keep their hold, the deer escaped and threw him quite out. Upon which his master, being in a great passion, and going to strike him, the honest old creature is said to have barked out this apology:—"Ah! do not strike your poor old servant; it is not my heart and inclination, but my strength and speed that fail me. If what I now am

displeases, pray don't forget what I have been."—Æsop's
Fables.

### ANECDOTE OF ALFRED THE GREAT.

Judith, mother-in-law of Alfred the Great, sitting one day amidst her husband's sons, is reported to have proposed a volume of Saxon poems, which she held in her hand as the prize of him who would first learn to read it. The elder princes remained untempted by this offer, but Alfred, who, though he had accompanied his father, Ethelwulf, to Rome and to the French Court, and was now in his twelfth year, was, like his brothers, unable to read, felt, unlike them, very anxious to gain the power of doing so, and having found a teacher, he, after due labour, acquired the book, by complying with the condition of being able to read it. From this time he became much addicted to study, but this did not render him inactive or slothful; on the contrary, he is eulogized as incomparably skilled in the chase, and almost recklessly brave in war.—Stories from English History (Hall.)

### THE MISER AND HIS FRIEND.

A miser said to a friend, "I have a sum of money which I want to take out from the city and bury; save to you I will not tell the secret to anyone." In short, both of them quitting the city deposited the coin under a certain tree. After several days the miser went alone to the spot, but found no trace of the gold. He said to himself, "Save that individual no one else knows the secret, but if I question him he will not confess." Accordingly he went to the man's house and said, "A great quantity of money has come into my possession, and I am desirous of depositing it in the same spot as before; if you will come to-morrow we will go together." The said friend in the desire after the larger sum, put back what he had carried off. Next day the miser repaired alone to the spot, where he found his money. Pleased with his plan, he never afterwards placed any reliance on the friendship of companions.—PERSIAN TALES.

### ANECDOTE OF THE EMPEROR JOSEPH II.

When the Emperor Joseph II. was in Paris, in the reign of Louis XVI., he was in the habit of walking about the city in disguise. One morning he went into an elegant hotel, and asked for a cup of coffee. He was plainly dressed, and the waiters insolently refused it, saying it was too early. Without making any reply, he walked out, and went into a little inn. He asked for a cup of coffee, and the host politely answered that it should be ready in a moment. While he waited for it, as the inn was empty, he walked up and down and was conversing on different subjects, when the landlord's daughter, a very pretty girl, made her appearance. The Emperor wished her "good morning," according to the French mode, and observed to her father that it was time she should be married. "Ah," replied the old man, "if I had but a thousand crowns, I could marry her to a man who is very found of her,—but sir, the coffee is ready." The Emperor called for pen, ink, and paper, which the girl ran and fetched: he gave her an order on his banker for six thousand livres.—ANON.

### FABLE—THE PEACOCK AND JUNO.

The peacock presented a memorial to Juno, importing how hardly he thought he was used, in not having so good a voice as the nightingale; how that pretty animal was agreeable to every ear that heard it, while he was laughed at for his ugly screaming noise, if he did but open his mouth. The goddess, concerned at the uneasiness of her favourite bird, answered him very kindly to this purpose. "If the nightingale is blest with a fine voice you have the advantage in point of beauty and largeness of person." "Ah," says he, "but what avails my silent unmeaning beauty, when I am so far excelled in voice!" The goddess dismissed him, bidding him consider that the properties of every creature were appointed by the decree of fate: to him beauty; strength to the eagle; to the nightingale a voice of melody; the faculty of speech to the parrot; and to the dove innocence. That each of these was contented with his own peculiar quality, and unless he had a mind to be miserable, he must learn to be so too.—Æsop's Fables.

### A RAVEN THAT ENTERTAINED THE CHICKENS.

There was a raven kept at an inn in the neighbourhood of Newhaven. This bird had been taught to call the poultry, and could do it very well too. One day—the table being set out for dinner—the cloth was laid, with the knives and forks, spoons and bread; and in that state it was left for some time, the room being shut, though the window was open. The raven had watched the operation very quietly, and as we may suppose, felt a strong ambition to do the like.

In due course of time the dinner was carried in—but, behold! everything had vanished from the table—silver spoons, knives, forks, all gone! But what was their surprise and amusement to see, through the open window, upon a heap of rubbish in the yard, the whole array very carefully set out, and the raven performing the honours of the table to a numerous company of poultry which he had summoned, about him, and was very grandly regaling with bread.—M. Howitt.

### SIR WILLIAM NAPIER AND THE LITTLE GIRL.

Sir William Napier was one day taking a long country walk, when he met a little girl about five years old sobbing over a broken bowl; she had dropped and broken it in bringing it back from the field, to which she had taken her father's dinner in it, and she said she would be beaten on her return home. Then, with a sudden gleam of hope, she looked up into his face, and said, "But you can mend it can you not?" Sir William smilingly explained that he could not mend the bowl, but he could give her sixpence to buy another. However, on opening his purse, it was empty of silver, and he had to make amends by promising to meet his little friend in the same spot at the same hour next day. The child entirely trusting him went on her way comforted. On his return home he found an invitation to dinner the following evening awaiting him, to meet some one whom he specially wished to see. He hesitated for some little time, trying to calculate the possibility of giving the meeting to his little friend of the broken bowl, and of still being in time for the dinner-party; but finding this could not be, he wrote to decline accepting the invitation on the plea of being engaged, saying to his family, "I cannot disappoint her, she trusted me so implicitly."— Anon.

### THE KING OF PERSIA AND THE BOY.

Thus it was that one of the kings of Persia—may God Most High watch over him—had a costly stone in a ring. Once, by way of recreation, he went out with some of his

principal officers into the public prayer ground of Shīrāz; he commanded (it), and so they put up the ring on the cupola of 'Azud's mausoleum, with the view that whoever should put an arrow through the circle of the ring, the ring should be his. It so happened that there were four hundred skilful archers in attendance on the monarch; they discharged their arrows, (and) all missed. But a boy who, on the roof of a caravansary, was shooting arrows in all directions, a favouring breeze carried his arrow through the circle of the ring. He obtained a robe of honour and money, and they gave him the ring. They relate that the boy burnt his bow and arrows. People said to him, "Why hast thou acted thus?" He replied, "In order that my first glory may remain intact."
It will sometimes happen that from a clear minded sage,
Not a single plan will come forth right;
At times it may be that a stupid boy
Will at random hit the target with his arrow."—GULISTAN.

### FABLE—THE EAGLE AND THE FOX.

An eagle that had young ones, looking out for something to feed them wherewith, happened to spy a fox's cub that lay basking itself abroad in the sunshine. She made a stoop, and trussed it immediately; but before she had carried it quite off, the old fox coming home, implored her with tears in her eyes, to spare her cub and pity the distress of a poor fond mother, who should think no affliction so great as that of losing her child. The eagle, whose nest was up in a very high tree, thought herself secure enough from all projects of revenge, and so bore away the cub to her young ones, without showing any regard to the supplications of the fox. But that subtle creature, highly incensed at this outrageous barbarity, ran to an altar, where some country people had been sacrificing a kid in the open fields, and catching up a firebrand in her mouth, made towards the tree where the eagle's nest was, with a resolution of revenge. She had scarce ascended the first branches, when the eagle, terrified with the approaching ruin of herself and family, begged of the fox to desist, and with much submission returned her the cub again safe and sound.—ÆSOP'S FABLES.

## BIRDS.

Those little nimble musicians of the air that warble forth their curious ditties with which nature hath furnished them to the shame of art.

As first the lark, when she means to rejoice, to cheer herself and those that hear her: she then quits the earth, and sings as she ascends higher into the air, and having ended her heavenly employment grows then mute and sad to think she must descend to the dull earth, which she would not touch, but for necessity.

\* \* \* \* \*

But the nightingale, another of my airy creatures, breathes such sweet loud music out of her little instrumental throat, that it might make mankind to think miracles are not ceased. He that at midnight, when the very labourer sleeps securely, should hear, as I have very often, the clear airs, the sweet descants, the natural rising and falling, the doubling and redoubling of her voice, might well be lifted above earth, and say, "Lord, what music has Thou provided for the saints in heaven, when Thou affordest bad men such music on earth?"—IZAAK WALTON.

## THE TRUMPETER AND THE HYENA.

One night, at a feast near the Cape of Good Hope, a trumpeter who had made himself intoxicated with liquor was carried out of doors and laid on the grass, in order that the air might both cool and sober him. The scent of the man soon attracted a spotted hyena, which threw him on his back, and carried him away towards the mountains. The hyena doubtless supposed that the senseless drunkard was a corpse, and consequently a fair prize.

In the meantime the musician awoke, and was at once sufficiently sensible to know the danger of his situation, and to sound his alarm with his trumpet which he fortunately carried at his side. The hyena, as it may be imagined, was greatly frightened in its turn, and immediately ran away, leaving the trumpeter, it is to be hoped a wiser man for his extraordinary ride. It is remarkable that the soldier was not seriously injured by the hyena, for the teeth of the animal were fortunately fastened in the coat and not in the flesh of the man.—
ANECDOTES IN NATURAL HISTORY. (MORRIS).

## THE COURTIER AND THE THIEVES.

In a certain city a quantity of wool was stolen; the owners thereof complained to the king, but much as His Majesty investigated the case, he could find no trace of the thief. A courtier said, "If you issue your decree I will catch the miscreant." The king gave him permission. The courtier went to his home, and on the pretence of a banquet, invited to his house high and low, small and great, of the city. When all the persons were collected together, the courtier came into the midst of the assembly, and casting his glance on the people said, "What base impudent fools those men are, who not only have stolen the wool, but come here with particles of wool in their beards." At the same instant several persons passed their hands through their beards, by which proceeding it became clear that they were the thieves.—PERSIAN TALES.

### FABLE—THE FOX AND THE STORK.

The fox invited the stork to dinner; and, being disposed to divert himself at the expense of his guest, provided nothing for the entertainment but soup in a wide shallow dish. This himself could lap up with a great deal of ease, but the stork, who could but just dip in the point of his bill, was not a bit the better all the while. However, in a few days after, he returned the compliment, and invited the fox; but suffered nothing to be brought to table but some minced meat in a glass jar, the neck of which was so deep and so narrow, that, though the stork with his long bill made a shift to fill his belly, all that the fox, who was very hungry, could do, was to lick the brims as the stork slabbered them with his eating. Reynard was heartily vexed at first; but when he came to take his leave, he owned ingenuously that he had been used as he deserved; and that he had no reason to take any treatment ill of which himself had set the example.—ÆSOP'S FABLES.

### KING CHARLES II. AND THE SUPPLIANT FOR OFFICE.

A gentleman in King Charles the Second's time, who had made numerous applications for an appointment at Court, and had received endless promises which were never carried out, at length resolved to see the king himself. Accordingly, having obtained an audience, he represented his claims to His Majesty, and boldly asked him for a certain post at the monarch's disposal. The king informed him that he had just given the appointment to another person. Upon which the gentleman thanked His Majesty most cordially, and expressed his gratitude in such a forcible manner, as to induce the king to inquire the cause of such profusion of thanks, on account of a case which had been refused. "Your courtiers," replied the gentleman, "kept me two years waiting, and gave me endless promises which they never fulfilled, but your Majesty has most generously told me the plain truth at once." "Thou hast answered discreetly," replied the monarch, "and thy request shall be granted."—ANON.

### FABLE—THE LION AND THE MOUSE.

A lion, faint with heat and weary with hunting, was laid down to take his repose under the spreading boughs of a thick shady oak. It happened that while he slept, a company of scrambling mice ran over his back and waked him. Upon which, starting up, he clapped his paw upon one of them, and was just going to put it to death when the little supplicant, begging him not to stain his noble character with the blood of so despicable and small a beast, the lion, considering the matter, thought proper to do as he was desired, and immediately released the little prisoner. Not long after, traversing the forest in pursuit of his prey, he chanced to run into the toils of the hunters; from whence, unable to disengage himself, he set up a most hideous and loud roar. The mouse, hearing the voice and knowing it to be the lion's, immediately repaired to the place and bid him fear nothing, for he was his friend. Then straight he fell to work, and with his sharp little teeth, gnawing asunder the knots and fastenings of the toils, set the royal brute at liberty.—ÆSOP'S FABLES.

### THE DEBTOR AND HIS CREDITORS.

A body of creditors brought a debtor before the judge, and said, "This man has received a large sum of money from us, and will not repay it." The judge enquired of him, "What answer do you give to this charge?" He replied, "They say truly, and their accusation is just; all I ask is such an amount of consideration as to enable me to sell my herd of camels, to pledge my gardens, and thereby satisfy their demands." The creditors exclaimed, "O sir! he is telling an utter untruth: he does not possess an atom of money, nor a span of land; neither is he the owner of a single sheep, much less of a herd of camels." The debtor rejoined, "O protector of the just! you now hear with your own ears their admission of my poverty and indigence, of what use is it to seek anything from a pauper?" The judge, turning to them, said, "The poor man is under the protection of God!" Accordingly, he delivered the clever debtor out of their hands.—PERSIAN TALES.

### SIR JOHN JERVIS AND THE DECOY VESSELS.

In the year 1796 Corsica was evacuated by the British, St. Fiorenzo being the last port they held on the island. The French had taken possession of the town and batteries, and all communication with the shore was suspended. The combined French and Spanish fleets were preparing to attack the British at anchor in the bay. Sir John Jervis had information that they meant to attack him by daylight on the following morning. So, as soon as it was dark, he despatched some light vessels of no use, to endeavour to escape by the eastward. They were seen by the enemy, who gave them chase, and separated their fleet. He then fastened a boat with a light suspended to the masthead at every buoy belonging to his ships, on board of which every light was carefully extinguished; and getting under sail, passed out of the gulf and clear of the enemy's fleet undiscovered; for, whilst part of them were engaged pursuing the light-vessels Sir John Jervis had sent as a decoy, the others were watching the lights in the bay, which they imagined to be those of the British fleet; and only when they bore down to make a certain conquest at daylight, discovered the trick that had deceived them.—LORD BYRON'S VOYAGE TO SICILY.

#### BEAR CATCHING IN RUSSIA.

In Russia there is a method of catching bears, by digging a pit several feet deep and covering it over with turf, sticks and leaves, upon the top of which a piece of flesh is placed. It may readily be supposed that the bear, as soon as he endeavours to seize the bait, tumbles into the pit. But it is a singular fact that if four or five happen to fall down together, they generally manage to escape by stepping on one another's shoulders, and thus reaching the top of the pit. But the ingenuity of the creatures is chiefly shown by their mode of extricating the last remaining comrade, who obviously cannot follow the example of his more fortunate brethren, there being no friendly shoulder whereon to mount. Accordingly, the sensible brutes run and fetch a large trunk of a tree, one end of which they place at the bottom of the pit, and make as it were a ladder, by means of which the confined bear effects his escape —ANON.

#### ANECDOTE OF DEAN SWIFT AND THE SERVANT.

A friend of Dean Swift one day sent him a fish as a present, by a servant who had frequently been on similar errands, but who had never received the most trifling mark of the dean's generosity. Having gained admission, he opened the door of the study, and abruptly putting down his charge cried very rudely, "Master has sent you a fish." "Young man," said the dean, rising from his easy chair, "is that the way you deliver your message? Let me teach you better manners. Sit down in my chair; we will change situations, and I will show you how to behave in future." The boy sat down, and the dean, going to the door, came up to the table with a respectful pace, and making a low bow said, "Sir, my master presents his kind compliments, hopes you are well, and requests your acceptance of a small present." "Does he?" replied the boy; "return my best thanks, and there is half-a-crown for yourself." The dean, thus drawn into an act of generosity, laughed heartily, and gave the boy a crown for his wit.—ANON.

### NATURE.

What variety of beautiful plants and flowers is there! which can be imagined to be of little other use but for the pleasure of man. And if man had not been, they would have lost their grace, and been trod down by the beasts of the field, without pity or observation; they would not have made them into garlands and nosegays. How many sorts of fruits are there which grow upon high trees, out of the reach of beasts! and, indeed, they take no pleasure in them. What would all the vast bodies of trees have served for, if man had not been to build with them, and made dwellings of them? Of what use would all the mines of metal have been, and of coal, and the quarries of stone? Would the mole have admired the fine gold? Would the beasts of the forest have built themselves palaces, or would they have made fires in their dens?—TILLOTSON.

### ANECDOTE OF A DOG.

During a severe storm a ship was wrecked on the beach, and every human being on board perished. The only living thing which escaped was a large dog of the Newfoundland breed, the property of the captain, which swam ashore, bringing in his mouth his master's pocket-book. He landed on the beach, whither he was driven by the heavy waves, amongst a number of spectators, several of whom endeavoured to take the pocket-book from him, but in vain. The sagacious animal, as if sensible of the importance of his charge, which had in all probability been delivered to him by his master in the hour of death, and when he saw all hope was gone, at length, after surveying the countenances of those assembled on the beach, leaped fawningly upon the breast of a man who had attracted his notice among the crowd, and delivered the pocket-book to him. The dog, immediately after depositing the rescued treasure into what he considered safe keeping, returned to the place where he had landed, and watched with great attention for everything that was drifted shorewards by the billows from the wrecked vessel, seizing it and endeavouring to bring it to land.—ANECDOTES OF DOGS.

### THE JUDGE'S MODE OF DETECTING DISHONESTY.

Two persons entrusted some property to an old woman, and said, "Whenever we both come back we will take it." After several days one of the parties went to the old woman and said, "My companion is dead, so now give me the money." She was helpless and gave it to him. Several days afterwards the other individual came, and demanded the property. The woman exclaimed, "Your comrade has been here, and represented that you were dead, and much as I protested, he would not hear a word, but carried off all the money." The man brought her before the judge, and demanded justice. The latter, after reflecting, ascertained that the woman was innocent. He decreed thus:—"You first made an agreement that whenever both you companions should come back you would demand the property—bring your comrade, and take the coin, why do you come alone?" The man was speechless, and departed.—PERSIAN TALES.

### ANECDOTE OF ST. ANTHONY.

St. Anthony, being in the wilderness led there a very hard and strict life, insomuch as none at that time did the like; to whom there came a voice from heaven, saying, "Anthony, thou art not so perfect as is a cobbler that dwelleth at Alexandria." Anthony hearing this, rose up forthwith, and took his staff and travelled till he came to Alexandria, where he found the cobbler. The cobbler was astonished to see so reverend a father come to his house. Then Anthony said unto him, "Come and tell me thy whole conversation, and how thou spendest thy time." "Sir," said the cobbler, "as for me, good works have I none, for my life is but simple and slender: I am but a poor cobbler; in the morning when I rise, I pray for the whole city wherein I dwell, especially for all such neighbours and poor friends as I have; after, I set me at my labour, where I spend the whole day in getting my living, and I keep me from all falsehood, for I hate nothing so much as I do deceitfulness; wherefore, when I make any man a promise, I keep it, and perform it truly; and thus I spend my time poorly with my wife and children, whom I teach and instruct, as far as my wit will serve me, to fear and dread God. And this is the sum of my simple life."—LATIMER.

### ANECDOTE OF AN ELEPHANT.

A female elephant, belonging to a gentleman at Calcutta, who was ordered from the upper country to Chittagong, in the route thither, broke loose from her keeper, and, making her way to the woods, was lost. The keeper made every excuse to vindicate himself, to which the master of the animal would not listen, but branded the man with carelessness, or something worse; for it was instantly supposed that he had sold the elephant. He was tried for it, and condemned to work on the roads for life, and his wife and children were sold for slaves. About twelve years afterwards, this man, who was known to be well acquainted with breaking elephants, was sent into the country with a party, to assist in catching wild ones. They came upon a herd, and this man fancied he saw amongst the group his long-lost elephant, for which he had been condemned. He resolved to approach it, nor could the strongest remonstrances of the party dissuade him from the attempt. Having reached the animal, he spoke to her, when she immediately recognised his voice; she waved her trunk in the air as a token of salutation, and spontaneously knelt down, and allowed him to mount her neck. She afterwards assisted in taking other elephants, and decoyed three young ones, to which she had given birth in her absence. The keeper returned, and the singular circumstances attending the recovery being told, he regained his character, and as a recompense for his unmerited sufferings, had a pension settled on him for life. This elephant was afterwards in possession of Warren Hastings, when Governor-General of Hindústán.
—Cassell's Natural History.

**NAPOLEON AND THE ARAB.**

When Napoleon was in Egypt, he wished to purchase of a poor Arab of the desert, a beautiful horse, with an intention of sending it to France as a present. The Arab pressed by want, hesitated a long time, but at length consented, on receiving a large sum of money in payment for the animal. Napoleon at once agreed to pay the sum named, and requested the Arab to bring his horse. The man, so indigent as to possess only a miserable rag as a covering for his body, arrived with his magnificent courser; he dismounted, and looking first at the gold and then steadfastly at the horse, heaved a deep sigh "To whom is it," he exclaimed, that I am going to yield thee up? To Europeans, who will tie thee up close, who will beat thee, who will render thee miserable! Return with me my beauty! my jewel! and rejoice the hearts of my children!" As he pronounced the last words, he sprang upon the animal's back, and was lost to sight in a moment. —ANON.

**FABLE—THE HARES AND THE FROGS.**

Upon a great storm of wind that blew among the trees and bushes, and made a rustling among the leaves, the hares (in a certain park where there happened to be plenty of them) were so terribly frightened that they ran like mad all over the place, resolving to seek out some retreat of more security, or to end their unhappy days by doing violence to themselves. With this resolution, they found an outlet where a pale had been broken down; and bolting forth upon an adjoining common had not run far before their course was stopped by that of a gentle brook, which glided across the way they intended to take. This was so grievous a disappointment, that they were not able to bear it, and they determined rather to throw themselves headlong into the water, let what would become of it, than lead a life so full of dangers and crosses. But upon their arriving at the brink of the river, a parcel of frogs, which were sitting there, frightened at their approach, leapt into the stream in great confusion, and dived to the very bottom for fear; which a cunning old puss observing, called to the rest and said, "Hold, have a care what ye do; here are other creatures, I perceive, which have their fears as well as us; don't, then, let us fancy ourselves the most miserable of any upon earth, but rather by their example learn to bear patiently those inconveniences which our nature has thrown upon us."—ÆSOP's FABLES.

### ABRAHAM AND THE TRAVELLER.

When Abraham sat at his tent door, according to his custom, waiting to entertain strangers, he espied coming towards him, an old man stooping and leaning on his staff, weary with age and travel, who was a hundred years of age. He received him kindly, washed his feet, provided supper, caused him to sit down; but observing that the old man eat and prayed not, nor begged for a blessing on his meat, he asked him why he did not worship the god of heaven; the old man told him that he worshiped the fire only, and acknowledged no other god; at which answer Abraham grew so zealously angry that he thrust the old man out of his tent, and exposed him to all the evils of the night and an unguarded condition. When the old man was gone, God called to Abraham, and asked him where the stranger was; he replied, "I thrust him away because he did not worship thee." God answered him, "I have suffered him these hundred years, although he dishonoured me, and couldst not thou endure him one night when he gave thee no trouble?" Upon this Abraham fetched him back again and gave him hospitable entertainment and wise instruction. Go thou and do likewise, and thy charity will be rewarded by the God of Abraham.—JEREMY TAYLOR.*

### KING RICHARD I. AND BLONDEL.

Blondel, the minstrel, seeing that his lord, King Richard I., did not return, though it was reported that he had passed the sea from Syria, thought that he was taken by his enemies, and probably very evilly treated; he therefore determined to find him, and for this purpose travelled through many countries without success; at last he came to a small town, near which was a castle belonging to the Duke of Austria, and, having learned from his host that there was a prisoner in the castle, who had been confined for upwards of a year, he went thither, and cultivated an acquaintance with the keepers. However, he could not obtain a sight of the prisoner, nor learn his quality; he therefore placed himself near to a window belonging to the tower wherein he was shut up, and sang a few verses of a song which had been composed conjointly by him and his patron. The king, hearing the first part of the song repeated the second, which convinced the poet that the prisoner was no other than Richard himself. Hastening, therefore, to England, he acquainted the barons with his adventure, and they, by means of a large sum of money, procured the liberty of the monarch.—STRUTT'S SPORTS AND PASTIMES.

* This story is taken from the Bústán of Shaikh Sa'dí.

## THE KING WHO FANCIED HIS MINISTER WAS GUILTY OF EXAGGERATION.

One day a king together with his minister went out for a walk, and arrived at a field where there were stalks of wheat as tall as a man. The king was much astonished and said, "I never saw wheat so tall as this." The minister replied, "My Lord! in my native country wheat grows as high as an elephant" The sovereign smiled, and the minister said to himself, "the king deems my words false, hence he smiles." When they had finished their walk he sent a letter to his friends in his own land asking for some stalks of corn; these, however, could not be gathered at the time the letter arrived, the harvest being over. In short, after a year some stalks of corn arrived. The minister went to the king, who demanded, "Why do you come here?" He represented, "Last year one day I stated that in my country corn grew to the height of an elephant, at which you smiled. I thought to myself that you doubted my assertion, so I have brought some stalks to verify my remark." The king said, "I now believe it, but beware not to make before any one a remark which cannot be verified till the lapse of a year."—PERSIAN TALES.

## SAGACITY OF A FOX.

A tame fox that was kept in a stable-yard was on very friendly terms with several of the dogs, but he could never induce the cats to come near him. Cats have very keen smell, and the odour arising from the fox was displeasing to them; they would not walk on any spot where he had been standing, and kept at as great a distance from him as possible. The fox soon saw the distaste of the cats to his company, so he made use of his knowledge to cheat them out of their breakfasts. As soon as their allowance of milk was poured out, he would run to the spot, and walk round the saucer, knowing that none of the cats would approach the defiled place. Day after day were the cats deprived of their milk; but the trick of the fox having been discovered, it was removed to some place where he could not get at it. The fox, not liking to be deprived of his morning draught, fell upon another plan for obtaining it. The dairymaid was in the habit of passing through the yard where the fox was, so he managed to go up to her and brush himself against one of the pails; the milk was immediately so tainted with the smell of the fox that the dairymaid did not venture to take it into the house, so she poured it out into a vessel and gave it to the cunning animal. He repeated this several times with success, but when the spoiled milk was given to the pigs, he left off troubling himself about it.—ANON.

### ANECDOTE OF DR. PALEY.

"I spent the two first years of my college life happily, but unprofitably. I was constantly in society, where we were not immoral, but idle and expensive. At the commencement of the third year, after having left the usual party at a late hour, I was awakened at five in the morning by one of my companions, who stood at my bedside and said, 'Paley, I have been thinking what a fool you are. I could do nothing, probably, if I were to try, and I could afford the indolent life you lead. You could do everything, and cannot afford it. I have had no sleep during the whole night on account of these reflections, and am now come solemnly to inform you that if you persist in your indolence, I must renounce your society.' I was so struck with the visit and the visitor that I lay in bed great part of the day, and formed my plan. I ordered my bed-maker to lay my fire every evening, in order that it might be lighted by myself. I arose at five, read during the whole day, took supper at nine, went to bed, and continued the practice up to this day." Such is Dr. Paley's own account of the reason which first led him to pursue his studies with energy, and turn to account the vast talents which for many years were concealed under a cloak of indolence and sloth.—ANON.

### FABLE—THE SHEPHERD AND HIS DOG.

A certain shepherd had a dog, upon whose fidelity he relied very much, for whenever he had an occasion to be absent himself, he committed the care and tuition of the flock to the charge of his dog; and to encourage him to do his duty cheerfully, he fed him constantly with delicate morsels, and sometimes threw him a crust or two more than usual. Yet, notwithstanding all this, no sooner was the man's back turned, but the treacherous cur fell foul upon the flock, and devoured the sheep, instead of guarding and defending them. The shepherd being informed of this, was resolved to hang him; and the dog, when the rope was about his neck, and he was just going to be tied up, began to expostulate with his master, asking him, why he was so unmercifully bent against him, who was his own servant and creature, and had only committed one or two crimes; and why he did not rather execute revenge upon the wolf, who was a constant and declared enemy? Nay, replies the shepherd, it is for that reason that I think you ten times more worthy of death than he; from him I expected nothing but hostilities, and therefore could guard against him; you I depended upon as a just and faithful servant, and fed and encouraged you accordingly; and therefore your treachery is the more notorious, and your ingratitude the more unpardonable.—ÆSOP's FABLES.

### TRUTH.

A young offender, whose name was Charlie Mann, broke a large pane of glass in a chemist's shop, and ran away at first, for he was slightly frightened; but he quickly began to think, "What am I running for? It was an accident; why not turn about and tell the truth?"

No sooner thought than done. Charlie was a brave boy; he told the whole truth—how the ball with which he was playing slipped out of his hand, how frightened he was, how sorry too, at the mischief done, and how willing to pay if he had the money.

Charlie did not have the money, but he could work, and to work he went at once in the very shop where he broke the glass. It took him a long time to pay for the large and expensive pane he had shattered, but when it was done, he had so endeared himself to the chemist by his fidelity and truthfulness that he would not hear of his going away, and Charlie became his clerk. "Ah, what a good day it was when I broke that window," he used to say.

"No, Charlie," his mother would respond, "what a good day it was when you were not afraid to tell the truth!"— ANON.

### FABLE—THE NIGHTINGALE AND THE HAWK.

A nightingale sitting all alone among the shady branches of an oak, sung with so melodious and shrill a voice, that she made the woods echo again, and aroused a hungry hawk, who was at some distance off, watching for his prey. He had no sooner discovered the little musician but, making a swoop at the place, he seized her with his crooked talons, and bid her prepare for death. "Ah!" says she, "for mercy's sake do not do so barbarous a thing, and so unbecoming to yourself. Consider, I never did you any wrong, and am but a poor small morsel for such a stomach as yours; rather attack some larger fowl, which may bring you more credit and a better meal, and let me go." "Ay!" says the hawk, "persuade me to do it if you can; I have been upon the watch all the day long, and have not met with one bit of anything till I caught you; and now you would have me let you go, in hopes of something better, would you? Pray, who would be the fool then?"—ÆSOP'S FABLES.

### ANECDOTE OF A SICK ELEPHANT.

An elephant at Calcutta had a disease in his eyes. For three days he was completely blind. His owner, an Engineer officer. asked my dear Dr. Webb if he could do anything to relieve the poor animal. The doctor said he would try the nitrate of silver, which was a remedy commonly applied to similar diseases in the human eye. The large animal was ordered to lie down, and at first, on the application of the remedy, raised a most extraordinary roar at the acute pain which it occasioned. The effect, however, was wonderful. The eye was in a manner restored, and the animal could partially see. The next day, when he was brought and heard the doctor's voice, he laid down of himself. placed his enormous head on one side, curled up his trunk, drew in his breath just like a man about to endure an operation, gave a sigh of relief when it was over, and then, by trunk and gesture, evidently wished to express his gratitude. What sagacity! what a lesson to us of patience!—BISHOP WILSON.

### LINES TO A NEWFOUNDLAND DOG.

When some proud son of man returns to earth,
Unknown to glory, but upheld by birth,
The sculptor's art exhausts the pomp of woe,
And storied urns record who rests below;
When all is done, upon the tomb is seen,
Not what he was, but what he should have been.
But the poor dog, in life the firmest friend,
The first to welcome, foremost to defend,
Whose honest heart is still his master's own;
Who labours, fights, lives, breathes for him alone,
Unhonour'd falls, unnoticed all his worth,
Denied in heaven the soul he held on earth.
While man, vain insect! hopes to be forgiven,
And claims himself a sole exclusive heaven.
Oh, man! thou feeble tenant of an hour!
Debased by slavery, or corrupt by power,
Who knows thee well must quit thee with disgust;
Degraded mass of animated dust!
Thy love is lust, thy friendship all a cheat,
Thy smiles hypocrisy, thy words deceit!
By nature vile, ennobled but by name,
Each kindred brute might bid thee blush for shame.
Ye! who perchance behold this simple urn,
Pass on—it honours none you wish to mourn:
To mark a friend's remains these stones arise;
I never knew but one,—and here he lies.—BYRON.

### THE WISE MAN AND THE CHEMIST.

A wise man entrusted a sum of money to a chemist, and went on a journey. After a while he returned, and

demanded back his gold. The chemist said, "You speak falsely, since you did not give me the property." The wise man laid hold of him, and men, collecting around them, charged the wise man with making a false accusation, and said, "This chemist is very upright, and never acted dishonestly; if you quarrel with him you will be punished." The wise man in despair wrote down the circumstances and submitted them to the king. The latter enjoined, "Go to the shop of the druggist, and remain there for three days, but say nothing to him; the fourth day I will go in that direction and salute you; save returning the compliment do not utter a word. When I leave the place demand your money from the chemist, and tell me what he says." The wise man, in accordance with the king's command, took his seat in front of the chemist's shop. The fourth day the king with a large retinue passed by that way, and when he saw the wise man he stopped his horse and saluted him; the latter saluted him in return. The king said, "Oh, brother! you never either come near me or tell me of your affairs." The wise man uttered not a word, but simply bowed his head. The chemist witnessed all this, and becoming alarmed, enquired of the wise man after the king had departed, "When you gave me the money, where was I, and who was present? repeat to me, maybe I have forgotten." The wise man recounted all the circumstances of the case. The chemist said, "You speak truly, now I remember." In short, he returned the money and humbly apologised.—
PERSIAN TALES.

## THE TWO GOLDFINCHES.

I have two goldfinches, which in the summer occupy the greenhouse. A few days since, being employed in cleaning out the cages, I placed that which I had in hand upon the table, while the other hung against the wall: the windows and the doors stood wide open. I went to fill the fountain at the pump, and on my return was not a little surprised to find a goldfinch sitting on the top of the cage I had been cleaning, and singing to, and kissing, the goldfinch within. I approached him, and he discovered no fear; still nearer, and he discovered none. I advanced my hand towards him, and he took no notice of it. I seized him, and supposed I had caught a new bird, but casting my eye upon the other cage perceived my mistake. Its inhabitant, during my absence, had contrived to find an opening, where the wire had been a little bent, and made no other use of the escape it afforded him than to salute his friend, and to converse with him more intimately than he had done before. I returned him to his proper mansion, but in vain. In less than a minute he had thrust his little person through the aperture again, and again perched upon his neighbour's cage, kissing him, as at first, and singing, as if transported with the fortunate adventure. I could not but respect such friendship, as for the sake of its gratification had twice declined an opportunity to be free, and consenting to their union, resolved that for the future one cage should hold them both.—COWPER.

### FABLE—THE COVETOUS MAN AND HIS AXE.

A man was felling a tree on the bank of a river, and by chance let slip out of his hand his hatchet, which dropped into the water, and immediately sunk to the bottom. Being, therefore, in great distress for the loss of his tool, he sat down and bemoaned most lamentably. Upon this Mercury appeared to him, and being informed of the cause of his complaint, dived to the bottom of the river, and coming up again, showed the man a golden hatchet, demanding if that were his. He denied that it was. Upon which Mercury dived a second time, and brought up a silver one. The man refused it, alleging likewise that this was not his. He dived a third time, and fetched up the individual hatchet the man had lost, upon sight of which the poor wretch was overjoyed, and took it with all humility and thankfulness. Mercury was so pleased with the fellow's honesty, that he gave him the other two into the bargain, as a reward for his just dealing. The man goes to his companions, and giving them an account of what had happened, one of them went presently to the river side, and let his hatchet fall designedly into the stream. Then sitting down upon the bank, he fell a weeping and lamenting, as if he had been really and sorely afflicted. Mercury appeared as before, and diving, brought him up a golden hatchet, asking if that was the hatchet he lost. Transported at the precious metal, he answered "Yes;" and went to snatch it greedily. But Mercury detesting his abominable impudence, not only refused to give him that, but would not so much as let him have his own hatchet again.—ÆSOP'S FABLES.

### THE DISPUTE BETWEEN THE HUNTING HAWK AND THE DOMESTIC FOWL.

Once upon a time a hunting hawk was engaged in a dispute with a domestic fowl, and beginning to contend, said, "You are a most faithless and treacherous bird; yet in fact, trustworthiness is the frontispiece of the page of acceptable manners; and in addition, fidelity is a perfect proof of religion; generosity and manliness, also, require that no one should inscribe the pages of his affairs with the mark of treachery."

The domestic fowl replied: "What ingratitude on my part have you seen, and what treachery have you observed?" The hawk answered: "The signs of your ingratitude are these—that, in spite of all the kindnesses which men show to you, without trouble or exertion on your part, apportioning you water and grain, from which the springs of life derive their existence; while day and night being apprised of your circumstances, they strenuously guard and watch you, and owing to their felicity you possess food and lodging, yet whenever they wish to catch you, you flee before and behind them, and fly from roof to roof, and run from corner to corner; while I, who am a wild animal, after having associated with them for two or three days only, and eaten food from their hands, keep in sight what is their due for this: hunting the game, I give it to them, and however far I may have gone, yet on merely hearing a call, flying, I come back." The fowl replied, saying, "You speak truly. Your return and my flight are owing to this, that you have never seen a hawk cooking on a spit, while I have beheld many domestic fowls roasting in a frying-pan. Were you ever to see such a sight, you would never come near them: and if I flee from roof to roof, you would hasten from hill to hill."—FABLES OF BIDPAI.

### THE ARAB AND HIS HORSE.

Giabal possessed a very excellent mare. Hassad Pasha, Vizier of Damascus, endeavoured to obtain it, but in vain. He employed threats, but with no success. At last another Bedouin, Giafar by name, came to the pasha, and asked him what he would give him if he brought to him Giabal's mare. "I will fill thy barley-sack with gold," was the Pasha's reply.

It was the practice of Giabal to fasten his mare at night by the foot with an iron ring, the chain of which passed into his tent, being held by a peg fixed in the ground, under the very felt which served him and his wife for a bed. At midnight, therefore, Giafar crept into the tent on all-fours, and insinuating himself between Giabal and his wife, pushed gently first the one and then the other. The husband thought his wife was pushing, she thought the same of her husband, so each made more room. Giafar then, with a knife, made a slit in the felt, took out the peg, untied the mare, mounted her, and grasping Giabal's lance, pricked him lightly with it, crying out, "It is I, Giafar, who have taken the noble mare; awake Giabal!" and off he went. Giabal darted from his tent, called his friends, mounted his brother's mare, and pursued the thief. Giabal's brother's mare was of the same breed as his own horse, but not so good. Outstripping all the other horsemen, he was on the point of overtaking Giafar, when he cried out, "Pinch her right ear, and give her the stirrup!" Giafar did so, and flying like lightning, was soon out of reach. The Bedouin reproached Giabal as having thus caused the loss of the mare. "I would rather," he said, "lose her, that injure her reputation. Would you have it said, in my tribe, that any other mare outran mine? I have the satisfaction of knowing that no other horse could overtake her—no, none!"—CASSELL'S NATURAL HISTORY.

### THE OLD MAN AND HIS ASS.

An old man and a little boy were driving an ass to the next market to sell. "What a fool is this fellow," says a man upon the road, "to be walking on foot with his son, that the ass may travel at ease." The old man hearing this set his boy upon the ass, and went whistling by the side of him. "Why, ho!" cried a second man to the boy, "is it fit for you to be riding, while your poor old father is walking on foot?" The father, upon this rebuke, took down his boy from the ass, and mounted himself. "Do you see," says a third, "how the lazy old knave rides along upon his beast, while this poor little boy is almost crippled with walking?" The old man no sooner heard this, than he took up his son behind him. "Pray, honest friend," says a fourth, "is that ass your own?" "Yes," says the man. "One would not have thought so," replied the other, "by your loading him so unmercifully. You and your son are better able to carry the poor beast than he you." "Anything to please," says the owner; and alighting with his son, they tied the legs of the ass together, and by the help of a pole endeavoured to carry him upon their shoulders over the bridge that led to the town. This was so entertaining a sight, that the people ran in crowds to laugh at it, till the ass, conceiving a dislike to the proceeding of his master, burst asunder the cords that tied him, slipped from the pole, and tumbled into the river. The poor old man made the best of his way home, ashamed and vexed that, by endeavouring to please everybody, he had pleased nobody, and lost his ass into the bargain.—ANON.

### FABLE—THE KITE AND THE PIGEONS.

A kite, who had kept sailing in the air for many days near a dove-house, and made a stoop at several pigeons, but all to no purpose (for they were too nimble for him) at last had recourse to stratagem, and took his opportunity one day to make a declaration to them, in which he set forth his own just and good intentions, who had nothing more at heart than the defence and protection of the pigeons in their ancient rights and liberties; and how concerned he was at their fears and jealousies of a foreign invasion, especially their unjust and unreasonable suspicions of himself, as if he intended, by force of arms, to break in upon their constitution, and erect a tyrannical government, over them. To prevent all which, and thoroughly to quiet their minds, he thought proper to propose to them such terms of alliance and articles of peace, as might for ever cement a good understanding betwixt them; the principal of which was, that they should accept of him as their king, and invest him with all kingly privilege and prerogative over them. The poor simple pigeons consented: the kite took the coronation oath after a very solemn manner on his part, and the doves the oaths of allegiance and fidelity on theirs. But much time had not passed over their heads, before the good kite pretended that it was part of the prerogative to devour a pigeon whenever he pleased. And this he was not content to do himself only, but instructed the rest of the royal family in the same kingly arts of government. The pigeons, reduced to this miserable condition, said, one to the other, " Ah! we deserve no better! Why did we let him come?"—ÆSOP'S FABLES.

### THE MERCHANT AND HIS BAD TEMPERED HORSE.

In former time there was a very intelligent merchant, who possessed a bad-tempered horse. One day this man was sitting eating his dinner at the threshold of his house. Meanwhile, a stranger came up riding on a mare, and, dismounting, was about to tie his mare beside the merchant's horse, and prepare to partake of some victuals he had with him. The merchant said to him, " Do not tie your mare near my horse, else you will meet with a loss; and do not eat beside me, or you will repent it." Hearing this, the man, nevertheless, tied his mare at that very spot, and sitting down beside the merchant, proceeded to eat his dinner. The latter said to him, "Who are you that without my invitation are eating along with me?" The stranger pretending to be deaf, made no reply. So the merchant thought he must be either deaf or dumb, and said no more. Meanwhile, his horse inflicted such a kick on the said mare, that she died. Then her owner began to quarrel with the merchant, saying, "Indisputably I shall exact the price of her from you; your horse has killed my mare." Thereupon the man went to the Kází (judge), and made a complaint. The Kází summoned the merchant before him. Accordingly he presented himself in Court, but feigned himself dumb. Whatever the judge asked him, he made no reply. The Kází said, "The man is dumb; it is no fault of his." The plaintiff said, "Your worship, how do you know that he is dumb? He told me at first that his horse was vicious, and that I must not tie my mare near him. Now he is pretending to be dumb!" The Kází said, "Tush! you are a rascally fool! you yourself attest that he warned you, and yet you make a claim for damages on account of your mare! What blame was there on his part in this case? Be off with you, out of my presence!" Accordingly, the judge had the man turned out of court, and dismissed the merchant.—TALES OF A PARROT.

### ANECDOTE OF SULTAN MAHMOUD.

We are told that the Sultan Mahmoud, by his perpetual wars abroad, and his tyranny at home, had filled his dominions with ruin and desolation, and half unpeopled the Persian empire. The vizier to this great Sultan pretended to have learnt of a certain dervis to understand the language of birds, so that there was not a bird that could open his mouth, but the vizier knew what it was he said. As he was one evening with the Sultan, on their return from hunting, they saw a couple of owls upon a tree that grew near an old wall out of a heap of rubbish. "I would fain know," says the Sultan, "what those two owls are saying to one another: listen to their discourse, and give me an account of it." The vizier approached the tree, pretending to be very attentive to the two owls. Upon his return to the Sultan, "Sir," says he, "I have heard part of their conversation, but dare not tell you what it is." The Sultan would not be satisfied with such an answer, but forced him to repeat, word for word, everything the owls had said. "You must know then," said the vizier, "that one of these owls has a son and the other a daughter, between whom they are now upon a treaty of marriage. The father of the son said to the father of the daughter, in my hearing, 'Brother, I consent to this marriage, provided you will settle upon your daughter fifty ruined villages for her portion.' To which the father of the daughter replied, 'Instead of fifty, I will give her five hundred, if you please. God grant a long life to Sultan Mahmoud; whilst he reigns over us we shall never want ruined villages.'"

The story says, the Sultan was so touched with the fable that he rebuilt the towns and villages which had been destroyed, and from that time forward consulted the good of his people.—SPECTATOR.

### THE DEAF MAN, THE BLIND MAN, AND THE WHIP.

Once upon a time, a deaf and a blind man alighted at a stage in one of the deserts. When early dawn appeared, and they were anxious to start, the blind man sought for his whip. By chance, a snake happened to lay there, stiffened by the cold; the blind man imagining it to be a whip, took it up; when he passed his hand over it, he discovered that it was softer and better than his own whip. Being on that account delighted, he mounted his horse, and forgot all about the whip which was lost. But when daylight appeared, the other man, who could see, looking, and observing a snake in the hand of the blind man, cried out, "O comrade! what you imagined to be a whip is a venomous snake: throw it from your hand before it can bite you." The blind man, fancying that his companion coveted the whip, replied, "O friend! as I have lost my own whip, the Creator has bestowed on me a better one. You also, if destiny befriends you, will find a nice whip; but I am not one of those from whose hands treachery and deceit can take my whip." The man who could see, smiled, and said, "O brother! the dues of companionship demand that I should apprise you of this danger; listen to what I say, and throw that snake from your hand." The blind man frowned, and said: "You have planned to get my whip, and are using every effort to induce me to throw it down, in the expectation that, after I have cast it aside, you will carry it off. Do not imagine such absurd ideas, and abandon such fruitless devices, since this is a whip come to my hands from the invisible world." Though the man who could see exerted himself to the utmost, and asseverated with deep and binding oaths, it was of no avail, and the blind man paid no attention to his words. Now, when the air became warm, and the snake lost his stiffness, he coiled himself about, and, in the midst of his writhings, inflicted a wound upon the hand of the blind man, who dropped down dead.—FABLES OF BIDPAI.

### SAGACITY OF A DOG.

Macaire, an officer of the body-guard of Charles V. of France, hated a comrade in the same service named Montdidier. Having met in the forest of Bondis, near Paris, Macaire treacherously murdered his brother officer, and buried him in a ditch.

Montdidier was unaccompanied except by a greyhound, which lay down on the grave of its master, and remained there until compelled by hunger to rise. It then went to the kitchen of one of Montdidier's dearest friends, where it was welcomed and fed. As soon as the dog's hunger was appeased, it was gone. For several days it went, and then disappeared, till at length the curiosity of those who saw its movements was excited, and it was resolved to follow the greyhound, and see if anything could be learned that would account for its master's sudden disappearance.

Accordingly, the dog was followed, and was seen to pause at some earth recently turned up, where its wailings and howlings became indescribably touching. Those who heard them now approached the spot, and, after digging for a time, found the corpse of Montdidier. It was speedily raised, and removed to Paris, where it was interred in one of the city cemeteries. The dog attached itself now to the friend of its late master. Several times it chanced to get a sight of Macaire, and on every occasion it sprang upon him, and would have strangled him, had it not been removed by force. It was evident that Montdidier had come by a violent death, and the hatred of his dog gave rise to a suspicion that Macaire had some share in his murder.

Charles V. on being informed of these circumstances, wished to satisfy himself of their truth. He caused

Macaire and the dog to be brought into his presence, and saw the animal again spring on the object of its hate. The king interrogated Macaire, but he would not admit that he had been concerned, in any way, in Montdidier's murder.

Convinced that the conduct of the dog was based on some guilty act of Macaire, the king ordered a combat to take place between the two, according to the practice in those times of deciding matters by wager of battle. The combat took place in the presence of the court. The king allowed Macaire to have a strong club, as a defensive weapon, while the only means of self-preservation allotted to the dog was a recess or hole, to which he might retreat on being hard pressed.

As soon as the combatants appeared in the lists the dog seemed perfectly aware of its position and duty. For a short time it leaped round Macaire, and then, with a determined spring, it fastened on his throat, so that he would have been strangled had he not cried for mercy, and confessed the crime. The dog was pulled from off him, but he only escaped its fangs to perish by the hand of the law.
—CASSELL'S NATURAL HISTORY.

### ROBINSON CRUSOE.

I was now in the twenty-third year of my residence in this island; and was so naturalised to the place, and the manner of living, that, could I have but enjoyed the certainty that no savages would come to the spot to disturb me, I could have been content to have capitulated for spending the rest of my time there, even to the last moment, till I had laid me down and died like the old goat in the cave. I had also arrived to some little diversions and amusements, which made the time pass a great deal

more pleasantly with me than it did before: as first, I had taught my parrot, as I noted before, to speak; and he did it so familiarly, and talked so articulately and plain, that it was very pleasant to me, for I believe no bird ever spoke plainer; and he lived with me no less than six-and-twenty years; how long he might have lived afterwards, I know not, though I know they have a notion in the Brazils that they live a hundred years. My dog was a very pleasant and loving companion to me for no less than sixteen years of my time, and then died of mere old age. As for my cats, they multiplied, as I have observed, to that degree, that I was obliged to shoot several of them at first, to keep them from devouring me and all I had; but at length, when the two old ones I brought with me were gone, and after some time continually driving them from me, and letting them have no provision with me, they all ran wild into the woods, except two or three favourites, which I kept tame, and whose young, when they had any, I always drowned; and these were part of my family. Besides these, I always kept two or three household kids about me, whom I taught to feed out of my hand; and I had two more parrots which talked pretty well, and would all call Robin Crusoe, but none like my first; nor, indeed, did I take the pains with any of them that I had done with him. I had also several tame sea-fowls, whose names I knew not, that I caught upon the shore, and cut their wings: and the little stakes which I had planted before my castle wall being now grown up to a good thick grove, these fowls all lived among these low trees, and bred there, which was very agreeable to me; so that, as I said above, I began to be very well contented with the life I led, if I could but have been secured from the dread of the savages.
—Defoe.

### ANECDOTE OF AN EAGLE.

A peasant with his wife and three children took up his summer quarters in a village, and pastured his flock on one of the rich Alpine mountains. The eldest boy was an idiot, about eight years of age; the second, five years old, but dumb; and the third an infant. One morning the idiot was left in charge of his brothers, and the three had wandered to some distance from the village before they were missed; and when the mother found the two elder, she could discover no trace of the babe.

A strange contrast was presented by the two children; the idiot seemed transported with joy, while the dumb brother was filled with consternation. In vain did the terrified parent attempt to gather from either what had become of the infant. But, as the idiot danced about in great glee, laughed immoderately, and imitated the action of one who had caught up something of which he was fond, and hugged it to his breast, the poor woman was slightly comforted, supposing that some acquaintance had fallen in with the children, and taken away the babe. But the day and the succeeding night passed without any tidings of the lost one. On the morrow the parents were earnestly pursuing their search, when, as an eagle flew over their heads, the idiot renewed his gesticulations, and the dumb boy clung to his father with frantic shrieks. Now the dreadful thought broke upon their minds that the infant had been carried off by a bird of prey, and that his half-witted brother was delighted at his riddance of an object which had excited his jealousy.

Meanwhile an Alpine hunter had been watching near a nest, hoping to shoot the mother-bird on returning to her home. At length, waiting with the anxious perseverance of such determined sportsmen, he saw her slowly flying towards the rock, behind which he had taken refuge, when on nearer approach, he heard, to his horror, the cries of an infant, and then beheld it in her frightful grasp. Instantly his resolve was made, to fire at the eagle the moment she should alight on the nest, and rather to kill the child than leave it to be devoured. With anxious heart he balanced, directed, and discharged his rifle; the ball went through the head and breast of the eagle; with indescribable delight he bore the babe away, and within a short time after it was missed, he had the satisfaction of restoring it—with wounds which were not serious on one of its arms and sides—to its happy mother's bosom.—CASSELL's NATURAL HISTORY.

### THE PORCUPINE, CHAMELEON, AND OWL.

One day a meeting took place between a porcupine and a chameleon, who entering into confidential discourse, each most bitterly complained of the scorn in which they were held by a cruel world. They both declared that they could not name one friend that they had in it, and yet could see no sufficient reason why they should be so badly treated, especially as they had sought by varied experiments to gain approbation, but still found to their cost that neither could succeed. In this dilemma they determined to apply to some competent judge to have the problem solved. They concluded that the owl was the proper object of their search, and accordingly presented themselves before him.

When the owl, having heard each eloquently make out his case, thus gave his judgment. First addressing the chameleon, "You," said he, "can lay no claim to friendship, since you only reflect back the object which is presented to you, as if you thought it a perfect model to imitate and worthy to engross the whole attention, like an insipid echo, offering neither advice, admonition, nor correction, but a mere servile flatterer, as you are, applauding equally whatever is presented to your notice—vice or virtue. And as to you," turning to the porcupine, "who hold yourself perpetually armed against all the world, and on every suggestion of envy or caprice shoot your sharp quills at friends or enemies, innocence or guilt, regardless who suffers while you enjoy the triumph of your power and the force of your weapons, what better fate can you expect than to be viewed with terror and dislike? Go, fretful porcupine, and base fawning chameleon, and if you cannot mend your manners, learn at least to be content without friends; for depend upon it, that none are without friends but those who deserve none."—NORTHCOTE'S FABLES.

### THE JUDGE AND THE MERCHANT'S PROPERTY.

A certain merchant left in his will seventeen horses to be divided among his three sons, according to the following proportions, viz., the first was to receive one half, the second one third, and the youngest one ninth part of the whole. But when they came to arrange about the division, it was found that to comply with the terms of the will without sacrificing one or more of the animals was impossible.

Puzzled in the extreme, they repaired to the Kázi (judge), who, having read the will, said that such a difficult question required time for deliberation, and recommended them to return in two days. When they again made their appearance the judge said:

"I have considered your case, and find that I can make such a division of the seventeen horses among you as will give each more than his strict share, and yet not one of the animals shall be injured. Are you content?"

"We are, O Kází," was the reply.

"Bring forth the seventeen horses, and let them be placed in the court-yard," said the Kází.

The animals were brought in, and the Kází ordered the groom to place his own horse with them.

He then bade the eldest brother to count the horses.

"There are eighteen in number, O Kází," he said.

"I will now make the division," responded the Kází. "You, the eldest, are entitled to half; then take nine horses: you, the second son, are to receive one third; take, therefore, six: while to you, the youngest, belongs the ninth part—namely two. Thus the seventeen horses are divided among you; you have each more than your share, and I may now take my own steed back again."

"O Kází!" said the brothers, "your wisdom equals that of our Lord Solomon!"—NOTES FROM NINEVEH.

### THE JACKAL WHO WAS ELECTED KING OF THE ANIMALS.

There was once a jackal that used constantly to go into a certain city, and to thrust his snout into every person's dish with the greatest impudence. Well, one night, according to custom, he entered the house of a certain indigo manufacturer; but, just as he was putting his nose into the vat, he fell into it, and his whole body was dyed indigo-colour. With the greatest difficulty he managed to clamber out again, and made off for the jungle. On account of his strange colour, the beasts of the forest did not recognise him, and supposing him to be some very distinguished animal, proposed to make him their king. Having so decided, the jackals accordingly elected him their king, and placed themselves entirely under his command. The jackal, now made chief, in order that no one might recognise him by his voice, made it his practice to place near him only the very smallest animals. Accordingly, whenever he held his court, he used to arrange them in the first rank, and the foxes in the second, the stags and monkeys in the third, the wolves in the fourth, the lions and tigers in the fifth, and the elephants in the sixth. Then he would say, "You all remain each in his own assigned position." And in the evening, when the jackals began to yelp, he indulged his natural tendency by yelping along with them, by which means he succeeded in not being recognised by any of the beasts.

After some days the elected chief, being angry with his brother jackals, dismissed them all from his immediate presence, and promoted the lions, tigers, and elephants to their post. As soon as it was night, the discarded jackals at a distance began their peculiar cry, and the chieftain himself, at his post of honour, joined them therein. The wild beasts which were standing around him, hearing the well-known voice, at once recognised his species, and were heartily ashamed. Without an hour's delay they made minced meat of him.—TALES OF A PARROT.

### ASEM THE RECLUSE.

Asem had spent his youth with men; had shared in their amusements; and had been taught to love his fellow-creatures with the most ardent affection; but from the tenderness of his disposition he exhausted all his fortune in relieving the wants of the distressed. The petitioner never sued in vain; the weary traveller never passed his door; he only hesitated from doing good when he had no longer the power of relieving.

From a fortune thus spent in benevolence he expected

a grateful return from those he had formerly relieved, and made his application with confidence of redress; the ungrateful world soon grew weary of his importunity, for pity is but a short-lived passion. He soon, therefore, began to view mankind in a very different light from that in which he had before beheld them; he perceived a thousand vices he had never before suspected to exist; wherever he turned, ingratitude, dissimulation, and treachery, contributed to increase his detestation of them. Resolved, therefore, to continue no longer in a world which he hated, and which repaid his detestation with contempt, he retired to this region of sterility, in order to brood over his resentment in solitude, and converse with the only honest heart he knew, namely, with his own.

A cave was his only shelter from the inclemency of the weather; fruits, gathered with difficulty from the mountains' side, his only food; and his drink was fetched with danger and toil from the headlong torrent. In this manner he lived sequestered from society, passing the hours in meditation, and sometimes exulting, that he was able to live independently of his fellow-creatures.—GOLDSMITH.

FABLE—THE COCK AND THE FOX.

A cock, being perched among the branches of a lofty tree, crowed aloud, so that the shrillness of his voice echoed through the wood and attracted a fox to the place, who was prowling in that neighbourhood in quest of prey. But Reynard, finding the cock was inaccessible, by reason of the height of his situation, had recourse to stratagem in order to decoy him down; so, approaching the tree, "Cousin," says he, "I am heartily glad to see you, but at the same time I cannot forbear expressing my uneasiness at the inconvenience of the place, which will not let me pay my respects to you in a handsome manner! though I suppose you will come down presently, and so that difficulty is easily removed." "Indeed, cousin," says the cock, "to tell you the truth I do not think it safe to venture upon the ground; for, though I am convinced how much you are my friend, yet I may have the misfortune to fall into the clutches of some other beasts, and what will become of me then?" "O dear!" says Reynard, "is it possible that you can be so ignorant as not to know of the peace that has been lately proclaimed between all kinds of birds and beasts; and that we are, for the future, to forbear hostilities on all sides, and to live in the utmost love and harmony, and that, under penalty of suffering the severest punishment that can be inflicted?" All this while the cock seemed to give little attention to what was said, but stretched out his neck, as if he saw something at a distance. "Cousin," says the fox, "what is it that you look at so earnestly?" "Why," says the cock, "I think I see a pack of hounds yonder, a little way off." "O then," says the fox, "your humble servant, I must be gone." "Nay, pray cousin do not go," says the cock, "I am just coming down; sure you are not afraid of dogs in these peaceable times?" "No, no," says he, "but ten to one whether they have heard of the proclamation yet."—ÆSOP'S FABLES.

### ADVENTURE WITH AN ALLIGATOR.

The ocean was very smooth and the heat very great, which made us so languid that almost a general wish overcame us on the approach of the evening, to bathe in the waters of the river. However, we were deterred from it by an apprehension of sharks, many of which we had observed in the course of the voyage, and these very large.

One man alone, who had been drinking too much, was

obstinately bent on going overboard, and, although we used every means in our power to persuade him to the contrary, he dashed into the water, and had swum some distance from the vessel when we on board discovered an alligator making towards him, behind a rock that stood a short distance from the shore. His escape seemed impossible, and one of the crew instantly seized a rifle to shoot the poor fellow ere he fell into the jaws of the monster. We waited with horror the event, and fired two shots at the approaching alligator, but without effect, for they glided off his skin, and the progress of the creature was by no means impeded. The noise of the gun soon made the man acquainted with his danger. He saw the creature making towards him, so with all his strength he swam for shore. On approaching within a very short distance of some caves and shoals that covered the bank, while closely pursued by the alligator, a ferocious tiger sprang towards him, at the instant that the jaws of his first enemy were extended to devour him. At this awful moment the man was preserved. The eager tiger, by overleaping, fell into the gripe of the alligator. A horrible conflict ensued. The water was coloured with the blood of the tiger, whose efforts to tear the skin of the alligator were unavailing, while the latter had also the advantage of keeping his adversary under water, by which the victory was presently obtained; for the tiger's death was now effected. They both sank to the bottom, and we saw no more of the alligator. The man was recovered, and instantly conveyed on board. He spoke not while in the boat, though his danger had completely sobered him; nor was he ever after seen the least intoxicated, nor did he ever again utter a single oath.—CASSELL'S NATURAL HISTORY.

### ALEXANDER SEVERUS AND HIS SOLDIERS.

Whilst Alexander Severus lay at Antioch, in his Persian expedition, the punishment of some soldiers excited a sedition in the legion to which they belonged. Alexander ascended his tribunal, and, with a modest firmness, represented to the armed multitude the absolute necessity, as well as his inflexible resolution, of correcting the vices introduced by his impure predecessor, and of maintaining the discipline which could not be relaxed without the ruin of the Roman name and empire. Their clamours interrupted his mild expostulation. "Reserve your shouts," said the undaunted emperor, "till you take the field against the Persians, the Germans, and the Sarmatians. Be silent in the presence of your sovereign and benefactor, who bestows upon you the corn, the clothing, and the money of the provinces. Be silent, or I shall no longer style you soldiers, but *citizens;* if those, indeed, who disclaim the laws of Rome, deserve to be ranked among the meanest of the people." His menaces inflamed the fury of the legion, and their brandished arms already threatened his person. "Your courage" resumed the intrepid Alexander "would be more nobly displayed in a field of battle: me you may destroy, but cannot intimidate: and the severest justice of the republic would punish your crime and revenge my death." The legion still persisting in clamorous sedition, the emperor pronounced with a loud voice the deserved sentence, "*Citizens!* lay down your arms, and depart in peace to your respective habitations." The tempest was instantly appeased; the soldiers, filled with grief and shame, silently confessed the justice of their punishment and the power of discipline, yielded up their arms and military ensigns, and retired in confusion, not to their camp, but to the several inns of the city. Alexander enjoyed during thirty days the edifying spectacle of their repentance, nor did he restore them to their former rank in the army till he had punished those tribunes whose connivance had occasioned the mutiny.—GIBBON.

### FABLE—THE FOX AND THE WOLF.

A wolf with hunger fierce and bold,
Ravaged the plains and thinned the fold;
Deep in the wood secure he lay,
By thefts at night regaled by day.
In vain the shepherd's wakeful care
Had spread the toils, and watched the snare;
In vain the dog pursued his pace,
The fleeter robber mocked the chase.
As Lightfoot ranged the forest round,
By chance his foe's retreat he found.
Let us a while the war suspend,
And reason as from friend to friend.
" A truce?" replies the wolf. 'Tis done.
The dog the parley thus begun:—
" How can that strong intrepid mind
Attack a weak defenceless kind?
Those jaws should prey on nobler food,
And drink the boar's and lion's blood.
Great souls with grievous pity melt,
Which coward tyrants never felt.
How harmless is our fleecy care!
Be brave and let thy mercy spare."
" Friend," says the wolf, " the matter weigh;
Nature designed us beasts of prey;
As such when hunger finds a treat,
'Tis necessary wolves should eat.

Hence, and thy tyrant lord beseech;
To him repeat the moving speech;
A wolf eats sheep but now and then,
Ten thousands are devoured by men.
An open foe may prove a curse,
But a pretended friend is worse.—GAY'S FABLES.

### ANECDOTE OF QUEEN MARGARET.

When the victorious soldiers of Edward IV. broke into their opponents camp, Margaret, queen of Henry VI. who had shortly before died, seized with mortal terror for the life of her child, fled with him on foot and alone into the neighbouring forest, where she pursued her way by the most unfrequented paths, in momentary dread of being overtaken by the enemy. Here she unhappily fell in with a band of robbers, who, attracted by the richness of her dress and that of the young prince, surrounded and despoiled them of their jewels and costly robes. While these ruffians were quarrelling about the division of their plunder, Margaret, with much courage and presence of mind, caught up her son in her arms, and fled to a neighbouring thicket, the robbers being too much occupied in fighting over the rich booty they had taken to observe her movements, favoured as they were by the inequalities of the ground.

When the shades of night closed round them, the fugitive queen and her son crept fearfully from their hiding place, and, uncertain whither to turn for refuge, began to attempt making their way through the forest, fearing above all things to fall into the hands of the foe. One wrong turn might lead them into the very midst of their enemies. While Margaret, bewildered with doubt and fear, was considering what was best to be done, she perceived by the light of the moon another robber approaching her, with his sword drawn. Gathering courage from the desperation of her case, the queen took her child by the hand, and presenting him to the ruffian she said, "Here is the son of your king, my friend—save his life!" A few words now explained to Margaret that the outlaw before her was a gentleman ruined in her husband's cause. He took the prince in his arms, and led the queen to his own retreat, a cave in Hexham Forest, still known by the name of "Queen Margaret's Cave," where the royal fugitives received such comfort and refreshment as the outlawed gentleman's wife could furnish.—STORIES FROM ENGLISH HISTORY (HALL).

### FABLE—THE WOLF AND THE MASTIFF.

A lean, hungry, half-starved wolf happened one moonshiny night to meet with a jolly, plump, well-fed mastiff; and, after the first compliments were passed, says the wolf, " You look extremely well, I protest, I think I never saw a more graceful, comely person: but how comes it about, I beseech you, that you should live so much better than I? I may say, without vanity, that I venture fifty times more than you do; and yet I am almost ready to perish with hunger." The dog answered very bluntly, " Why, you may live as well, if you will do the same for it that I do." " Indeed! what is that?" says he. " Why," says the dog, "only to guard the house a-nights, and keep it from thieves." " With all my heart," replies the wolf: " for at present I have a sorry time of it, and I think to change my hard lodgings in the woods, where I endure rain, frost, and snow, for a warm roof over my head, and a bellyful of good victuals, will be no bad bargain." " True," says the dog, " therefore you have nothing more to do than to follow me." Now, as they were jogging on together the wolf espied a crease in the dog's neck, and, having a strange curiosity, could not forbear asking him what it meant. "Pugh! nothing," says the dog. "Nay, but pray," says the wolf. "Why," says the dog, "if you must know, I am tied up in the day-time, because I am a little fierce, for fear I should bite people, and am only let loose at night. But this is done with the design to make me sleep a-days, more than anything else, and that I may watch the better in the nighttime; for, as soon as ever the twilight appears, out I am turned, and may go where I please. Then my master brings me plates of bones from the table with his own hands; and whatever scraps are left by any of the family, all fall to my share; for you must know I am a favourite with everybody. So, you see how you are to live. Come, come along; what is the matter with you?" "No," replied the wolf, "I beg your pardon, keep your happiness all to yourself. Liberty is the word with me, and I would not be a king on the terms you mention."—Æsop's Fables.

### A RAVEN THAT WENT TO A FAIR.

There was, some years ago, a cunning, mischievous raven, named Ralph, kept at a lonesome farm-house in Derbyshire. He was a great favourite with all the family, though he often created much annoyance and trouble by his thievish tricks. Whatever came in his way, which was not too heavy for him to lift, he carried off; yet, though everyone knew who was the thief, he seldom came in for punishment, the servants and different members of the family being blamed instead, for leaving things in his way. Notwithstanding the care, however, which everybody took to put things in their places, Ralph found many a little article, of which he made a prize, and many a one which was never missed at the time.

After Ralph had practised his thievery, and indulged his habit of secretiveness for some years, all his hoard came one day suddenly to light. He had buried it in, as he had thought, a cunning hole, that he had made in the thatched roof of a barn. His treasure grew and grew, and the hole had been deepened and deepened, till it was deep as the thatch itself, and then all his accumulations fell through upon the barn floor. And what a wonderful accumulation there was! There was a world of amusement in the owning of Ralph's treasury, and many an old forgotten thing was brought to light, and many another was found of which nobody could give an account.

The winter after this event poor Ralph came to an untimely end. The travelling tailor who used to come now and then to the house to make and mend the clothes of the family, had made him, of scarlet cloth, a comb like a cock, which the creature allowed to be put on, and seemed to wear with as much pride as a young soldier wears his new uniform. Not long after being thus decked, there chanced to be a fair in the neighbourhood, and, as several of the members of the family went to it, Ralph saw no reason why he might not go also. Off, therefore, he flew after them, and arriving in the middle of the fair, perched upon the roof of a house, which stood in the centre of the place. The poor fellow, gaily decked, was immediately descried, everybody taking him for some wonderful bird, and everybody being desirous of securing him.

Unfortunately, a man with a gun was at hand, and to make sure of so strange a creature while he was within reach, fired at him, and poor Ralph fell mortally wounded. Hardly had he reached the ground, when his old friends of the farm came up with a crowd that had been drawn to the spot by the firing of the gun, and in the strange creature they instantly recognized their old favourite. Great was the lamentation that was made over him, and loud and vehement their indignation against the culprit who had thus ended his days. His sagacity was an endless theme of discourse; story after story was told of him, and so great was the sympathy of all the people, that for some time they forgot the amusements that surrounded them, to condole over the unfortunate raven that came to the fair in all his finery, to meet so tragic an end.—M. HOWITT.

### FABLE—THE FOOLISH YOUNG COCK.

As an old hen led forth her train,
And seemed to peck to shew the grain,
She raked the chaff, she scratched the ground,
And gleaned the spacious yard around.
A giddy chick, to try her wings,
On the well's narrow margin springs,
And prone she drops. The mother's breast
All day with sorrow was possest.
A cock she met; her son she knew;
And in her heart affection grew.
" My son," says she, " I grant your years
Have reached beyond a mother's cares.
I see you vigorous, strong, and bold;
I hear with joy your triumphs told.
'Tis not from cocks thy fate I dread,
But let thy ever wary tread
Avoid yon well; that fatal place
Is the sure ruin of our race."
He thanked her care, yet day by day
His bosom burned to disobey,

And every time the well he saw,
Scorned in his heart the foolish law.
Near and more near each day he drew,
And longed to try the dangerous view.
" Why was this idle charge?" he cries:
" Let courage female fears despise.
Or did she doubt my heart was brave,
And therefore this injunction gave?
Or does her harvest store the place,
A treasure for her younger race?"
And would she thus my search prevent?
I stand resolved, and dare the event."
Thus said, he mounts the margin's round,
And peers into the depth profound.
He stretched his neck; and from below
With stretching neck advanced a foe;
With wrath his ruffled plumes he rears,
The foe with ruffled plumes appears:
Threat answered threat; his fury grew;
Headlong to meet the war he flew;
But, when the watery death he found,
He thus lamented as he drowned:
" I ne'er had been in this condition
But for my mother's prohibition."—GAY's FABLES.

### ANECDOTE OF A CAT.

A favourite cat that was accustomed from day to day to take her station quietly at my elbow, or the writing table, sometimes for hour after hour, whilst I was engaged in study, became at length less constant in her attendance, as she had a kitten to take care of. One morning she placed herself in the same spot, but seemed unquiet, and, instead of seating herself as usual, continued to rub her furry sides against my hand and pen, as though resolved to draw my attention and make me leave off.

As soon as she had accomplished this point, she leaped down on the carpet and made towards the door, with a look of great uneasiness. I opened the door for her, as she seemed to desire; but, instead of going forward, she turned round and looked earnestly at me, as though she wished me to follow her, or had something to communicate. I did not fully understand her meaning, and, being much engaged at the same time, shut the door upon her, that she might go where she liked. In less than an hour afterwards she had again found an entrance into the room, and drawn close to me; but, instead of mounting the table and rubbing herself against my hand as before, she was now under the table, and continued to rub herself against my feet; on moving which I struck them against something which seemed to be in their way, and, on looking down, beheld, with equal grief and astonishment, the dead body of her little kitten, covered over with ashes, and which I supposed had been alive and in good health.

I now entered into the entire train of this afflicted cat's feeling. She had suddenly lost her beloved kitten, and was resolved to make me acquainted with it—assuredly that I might know her grief, and probably, also, that I might inquire into the cause; and finding me too dull to understand her expression, motioning that I would follow her to the spot where the dead kitten had been thrown, she took the great labour of bringing it to me herself, and laid it at my feet. I took up the kitten in my hand, the cat still following me, made inquiry into the cause of its death, which I found, on summoning the servants, to have been an accident, in which no one was much to blame: and the fond mother, having thus obtained her object, and got her master to enter into her cause, and divide her sorrows with her, gradually took comfort, and resumed her former station by my side.—CASSELL'S NATURAL HISTORY.

### THE HORATII AND CURIATII.

Tullus Hostilius, a man of brave and warlike character, was chosen to succeed Numa. Disputes soon began to arise between Rome and Alba; their peace-maker was no more, and each side prepared for war. King Tullus proposed to the Alban general to end the quarrel by a single combat between themselves; but the general, who it seems was not remarkable for personal courage, proposed to select three champions from each camp, who might decide the dispute, and spare the lives of the chiefs. Tullus accepted the proposal.

There was great emulation among the young warriors for the honour of being chosen a champion on this occasion. Three brothers were selected from each army, remarkable for strength and dexterity in the use of their weapons. Horatius, the father of the Roman youths, left them to follow their own inclinations, and, being informed of their resolution to accept the challenge, embraced them, and lifting up his eyes to heaven, exclaimed, "I am a happy father!"

On the day appointed for the combat the several champions appeared upon the plain between the two armies, each to meet his adversary. At the moment that the spectators expected to see them engage in fierce encounter, they quitted their arms, and ran to embrace each other.

Charmed with the action, and grieved that such generous spirits should waste their lives in rivalry so cruel, the people began to murmur at their kings; but a new scene claimed their attention. The combat began, and long continued equal. The eldest of the Horatii at length received a mortal wound; the second shared the same fate, and expired upon the body of his brother. The Alban army raised shouts of exultation, while despair spread amid the Roman camp. Such hope as bloodshed and death can afford yet rested upon the Alban brothers being all wounded, while the third of the Roman youths was still unhurt and undaunted.

Unable to sustain the attacks of three at one time, the Roman youth pretended fear, and hastily fled before his pursuers, endeavouring to separate them—he succeeded—he turned round upon the first and slew him; the second shared the same fate. The third was in no condition to fight, being scarcely able to support himself on his shield. Horatius exclaimed, "To the glory of Rome I sacrifice thee!" and thus perished the last of the three Curiatii.—STORIES FROM THE HISTORY OF ROME.

### THE TAME BEAR.

Some years ago a boy of New Hampshire found a very young bear near Lake Winnipeg, and carried it home with him. It was fed and brought up about the house of the boy's father, and became as tame as a dog.

Every day its youthful captor had to go to school at some distance, and by degrees the bear became his daily companion. At first the other scholars were shy of the creature's acquaintance; but ere long it became their regular playfellow, and they delighted in sharing with it the little store of provisions which they brought for their sustenance in small bags. After two years of civilisation, however, the bear wandered to the woods, and did not return. Search was made for him, but in vain.

Four succeeding years passed away, and in the interval

changes had occurred in the school alluded to. An old lady had succeeded the ancient master, and a new generation of pupils had taken the place of the former ones. One very cold winter day, while the schoolmistress was busy with her humble lessons, a boy chanced to leave the door half-way open on his entrance, and suddenly a large bear walked in.

The consternation of the old lady and her boys and girls was unspeakable. Both schoolmistress and pupils would fain have been abroad; but the bear was in the path, and all that could be done was to fly off as far as possible behind the tables and benches. But the bear troubled them. He walked quietly up to the fireplace and warmed himself, exhibiting much satisfaction in his countenance during the process.

He remained thus about a quarter of an hour; and then walked up to the wall where the bags and baskets of the pupils' food were suspended. Standing on his hind feet he took hold of these successively, put his paws into them, and made free with the bread, fruit, and other eatables therein contained. He next tried the schoolmistress's desk, where some little provisions usually were, but finding it firmly shut, he went up again to the fire, and, after a few minutes' stay before it, he walked out by the way he entered.

As soon as the schoolmistress and her pupils had courage to move, the alarm was given to the neighbours. Several young men immediately started after the bear, and, as its track was perfectly visible upon the snow, they soon came up with it and killed it. Then it was that by certain marks upon its skin some of the pursuers recognized the old friend of their school-days. Great regret was felt at the loss of the creature. It was like killing a human friend rather than a wild animal.—ANECDOTES IN NATURAL HISTORY.

## THE FLEA, THE GRASSHOPPER, AND THE CRICKET.

The flea, the grasshopper, and the cricket, had once a mind to see who could leap the highest, so they invited the whole village, and whomsoever else might choose to come, to see the sight. And three famous jumpers they were, who were assembled in the room.

"I will give my daughter to whichever leaps the highest," said the king; "for it would be too bad if these folks jumped for nothing."

The flea came first. His manners were very elegant, and he bowed to everybody, for he had noble blood in his veins, and was accustomed to the society of human beings, which makes all the difference.

Then came the grasshopper, who was certainly somewhat heavier, yet displayed a good figure that was set off by a becoming green dress. Moreover, this personage maintained that he belonged to a very ancient family in Egypt, where he was thought very highly of. He had just been taken out of a field and put into a summer-house, made of playing cards, with the figured sides turned inwards. "I sing so well." said he, "that sixteen native crickets who had whistled from their early youth without being able to obtain a summer-house, fretted themselves still thinner than they were already, when they heard me."

Both the flea and the grasshopper duly proclaimed who they were, and that they considered themselves fit to marry a princess.

The cricket said nothing, but he did not think the less, it is said, and when the watch dog had merely sniffed him, he answered for it that the cricket was of good family, and was made out of the breastbone of a real goose. The old senator, who had obtained three orders for holding his tongue, maintained that the cricket was endowed with the faculty of prophecy, and that one could tell by his voice whether the winter would be mild or severe.

"Ay, I say nothing," observed the old king; "but I go my own ways, and have my own thoughts like other people."

And now the leap was to be taken. The flea jumped so high that nobody could see so far, and therefore they maintained that he had not leaped at all, which was quite contemptible on their parts.

The grasshopper only leaped half as high, but jumped right into the king's face, which his majesty said was not pretty behaviour.

The cricket stood still a long while, and was lost in thought, and people began to think at last that he could not jump at all.

"It is to be hoped he is not ill," said the watch dog, smelling him once more; when away he sprang, with a little sideways jerk, into the lap of the princess, who was sitting modestly on a golden stool.

Then the king said, "The highest leap is the one that aimed at my daughter, for that implies a delicate compliment. It wanted some head to hit upon such an idea: and the cricket has shown that he has a head."

So he obtained the princess.

The flea for all that maintained that he had jumped the highest, so he went into foreign lands, and it is said got killed, while the grasshopper sat outside in a ditch musing over his misfortune and singing his melancholy song.—
ANDERSEN'S TALES.

### THE WRESTLER AND HIS PUPIL.

A certain one had arrived at perfection in the art of wrestling; for he used to know three hundred and sixty excellent sleights in his art, and daily wrestled after a new fashion. But his innermost heart was inclined towards the beauty of one of his pupils. He taught him three hundred and fifty-nine manœuvres, (all in fact) except one artifice, the teaching of which he put off with excuses, and deferred. In brief, the youth reached the farthest limit of strength and skill, and no one was able to contend with him; so much so, that he one day said, in the presence of the king of the time, "The superiority which my master enjoys over me is (allowed him) in consideration of his age and the claims of training; otherwise, I am not inferior to him in strength, and in skill I am equal to him." These words sounded harsh and displeasing to the king; he commanded that they should wrestle. They got ready a spacious arena, and the lords and distinguished nobles of the court, together with all the athletes of the world, were in attendance. The youth advanced like a mad elephant, with a shock that, had there been a mountain of iron it would have torn it up from its base. The master knew that the young man was superior to him in strength, and equal in skill; he closed with him with that strange artifice which he had kept concealed from him. The youth knew not how to meet it. The master lifted him with both hands from the ground, and raised him above his head, and flung him to the ground. A shout arose from the multitude. The monarch commanded them to bestow a robe of honor and a reward of money on the tutor, and himself scolded and rebuked the youth, saying, "Thou presumedst to encounter thine own tutor, and failed to make good thy pretension." The youth said, "My lord! my master did not triumph over me by strength; but a nice point in wrestling which he had withheld from me was wanting to me; to-day he got the better of me by that nice point." The master said, " I reserved it for such a day as this; for the sages say, ' Give not a friend so much power that, if he should prove hostile, he may be able to do so.' Hast thou not heard what he said who suffered wrong from a pupil of his own?"

'I taught him archery every-day,
And when his arm waxed strong, he shot me.'—GULISTAN.

### THE RESULT OF AVARICE.

In the city of Balkh there once lived four wealthy persons, mutual friends. It so happened, however, that all four became poor, and in their distress they applied to a certain sage for his advice. To him each of them told his own story. The sage compassionated them, and giving to each of them a talisman, said, " Each of you put your respective charm upon your head and go your way. On whatever spot it falls, let him dig there, and whatever casts up will belong to him." Accordingly all four, having thereupon placed each his talisman on his head, took their departure, all in the same direction.

When they had gone several miles, the talisman of one fell from his head. He then dug on the spot and found copper. " I consider this copper!" said he to the other three, " as better than gold; if you like, you can all remain here with me." They did not accept his invitation, but went on. They had not gone far, when the talisman fell from the head of a second, who, on digging in the ground, found silver. Then he likewise said to the other two, " you remain with me. The silver is abundant, we might all make a livelihood out of it; each of you consider it as his own as much as mine." However they did not take his advice, but went on till the talisman of the third fell from his head, and when he, too, dug up the ground, lo! gold was found. Delighted with his luck, he said to the fourth, "Well, now, there can be nothing better than this. I should like much for us both to remain here." But he replied, "No, I will go on, and probably I shall find a mine of jewels; why should I stay here?" So saying, he proceeded forwards; when he had got about ten miles farther, his talisman also fell, and on his likewise digging in the ground, iron made its appearance. Seeing this result, he was exceedingly chagrined, and said to himself, "Why did I leave the gold, and not take my friends advice?" So abandoning the iron, he went in search of his companion, who had discovered the gold mine, but he neither found him nor his gold. Then he went after the man with the silver, but could not find him either; and from thence he went where he had left the copper discoverer, but him, also, he failed to find. Then bewailing his destiny, he said, "No man ever yet got beyond what he was predestined to obtain." At last he went to the sage's home, but even him he did not find there. The poor fellow, overwhelmed with remorse, reproached himself with his avarice, which had brought him to such straits.—TALES OF A PARROT.

### INVASION OF ENGLAND BY THE DANES.

A Danish chieftain of high rank, some say of royal blood, named Lothbroc, amusing himself with his hawk near sea, upon the western coasts of Denmark, the bird, in pursuit of her game, fell into the water; Lothbroc, anxious for her safety, got into a little boat that was near at hand, and rowed from the shore to take her up, but before he could return to the land, a sudden storm arose, and he was driven out to sea. After suffering great hardship, during a voyage of infinite peril, he reached the coast of Norfolk, and landed at a port called Rodham; he was immediately seized by the inhabitants, and sent to the court of Edmund, King of the East Angles; when the monarch was made acquainted with the occasion of his coming, he received him very favourably, and soon became particularly attached to him, on account of his great skill in the training and flying of hawks. The partiality which Edmund manifested for this unfortunate stranger, excited the jealousy of Beoric, the king's falconer, who took an opportunity of murdering the Dane, whilst he was exercising his birds in the midst of a wood, and secreted the body, which was soon after discovered by the vigilance of a favourite spaniel. Beoric was apprehended and, it seems, convicted of murder; for he was condemned to be put into an open boat without oars, mast, or rudder, and in that condition abandoned to the mercy of the ocean. It so chanced, that the boat was wafted to the very point of land that Lothbroc came from, and Beoric, escaped from the danger of the waves, was apprehended by the Danes, and taken before two of the chieftains of the country, who were both of them sons of Lothbroc. The crafty falconer soon learned this circumstance, and, in order to acquire their favour, made them acquainted with the murder of their father, which he affirmed was executed at the command of King Edmund, and that he himself had suffered the hardship at sea, from which he had been delivered by reaching the shore, because he had the courage to oppose the king's order, and endeavoured to save the life of the Danish nobleman. Incited by this abominable falsehood to revenge the murder of their father, by force of arms, they invaded the kingdom of the East Angles, pillaged the country, and having taken the king prisoner, caused him

to be tied to a stake and shot to death with arrows.—
STRUTT'S SPORTS AND PASTIMES.

### ANECDOTE OF A CROSSING SWEEPER.

In the first quarter of this century there lived in London an old man who used to sweep a crossing, of whom a very singular story is told. This old crossing-sweeper, whatever was the amount of the alms bestowed upon him, always used only to retain a halfpenny and return the rest to the donor. This very strange custom having become known procured him many halfpennies. It happened one day that a gentleman who was in the habit of going frequently to London on business, was surprised by a heavy shower while in the streets. He took refuge under an archway, and had stood there for some time waiting for the storm to clear away, when the door of a handsome house opposite was opened, and a servant with an umbrella in his hand, crossed the street, and presenting his master's compliments, requested the gentleman to take shelter in the house. He gladly accepted the invitation, and following the man, was ushered into a handsomely furnished room, where he was received by the master of the house.

The gentleman was struck at once with a vague recollection of having seen the same person before, but where, or under what circumstances, he was unable to recall to mind. His inquiring glances during their conversation did not escape his host. "You seem, sir," said he at last, "to look at me as if you had seen me before." He replied that he thought such was the case, but that he could not recall the occasion. "You are right, sir," replied the host, "and if you will pledge your word of honour to keep my secret until you have seen the notice of my death in the papers,

I have no objection to remind you where and when you have seen me."

He then said that he was the crossing-sweeper who never accepted more than one halfpenny. "Many years ago," he added, "I first hit upon this expedient for the relief of my then pressing necessities. I was at that time destitute, but finding the scheme to answer beyond my expectations, I was led to carry it on, until I had at last realised a handsome fortune, enabling me to live in the comfort in which you find me to-day. And now, sir, such is the force of habit, that though I am no longer under any necessity for continuing this plan, I find myself quite unable to give it up. Accordingly, every morning I leave home, apparently for business purposes, go to a room where I put on my beggar's clothes, and continue sweeping my crossing till a certain hour in the afternoon, when I go back to my room, resume my usual dress, and return home in time for dinner, as you see me this day."—STORY OF THE LONDON PARKS.

### THE NOBLEMAN AND THE SERPENT.

One day a certain nobleman, having gone to hunt in a forest, was surprised to see a black serpent come right up to him, and thus address him:—"O nobleman! for God's sake give me some place where I may hide myself, and I will bless you for it!" The *Amir* \* asked, "why are you so alarmed? is there anything wrong?" The snake replied, "My enemy is coming along, club in hand, to kill me. Do conceal me somehow!" On hearing this, the *Amir* took compassion on the animal, and concealed it in his wide sleeve. After a while, the person referred to by the snake, came up, armed with a thick bamboo pole, and said, "A black serpent, fleeing before me, has just

\* Nobleman, or chief.

come in this direction. Tell me, if you have seen it. I will smash its head with this bamboo, and then make my way home." Upon this, the *Amír* said, " I have been standing here, friend, for a long while, but have seen nothing of the kind. God only knows where it has gone." Then the man made much search for the animal all round about, but not finding it, set out for home.

About an hour after, the *Amír* said to the snake, "Your enemy has gone, so now you go too!" The serpent laughed, and replied, "My good sir, I will not leave now without stinging you! Do you think I am going to listen to you, and move off without anyone being killed? Are you so ignorant about me as not to know that I am your natural enemy? When I have killed you, then I will go, but not before. You are evidently an egregious fool, to have taken compassion on me, and, believing what I told you, given me a place in your sleeve!" Then the *Amír* said, "Serpent, I have done a kindness to you, and you intend to requite it with evil! This is very improper!" "I have heard from wise men," rejoined the snake, "that to do good to the bad is just like doing harm to the good." On hearing this, the man was greatly afraid, and said to himself, "How shall I get him out of my sleeve, and preserve my life?" After reflection, he determined on an expedient, and said to the animal, "Black snake, there is another serpent coming; you get out of my sleeve, and then you and I will both go and ask its opinion. If it approves of your design, then do with me as you like." Finally, the snake agreed to his proposal, and, coming out of his sleeve, went towards the other snake. Whereupon the *Amír* seizing the opportunity, struck it such a blow on the head with a stone, as to kill it. And thus he succeeded in getting safe home—TALES OF A PARROT.

## THE TWO SHEPHERDS.

When the plains of India were burnt up by a long continuance of drought, Hamet and Raschid, two neighbouring shepherds, faint with thirst, stood at the common boundary of their grounds, with their flocks and herds panting round them, and in extremity of distress prayed for water. On a sudden the air was becalmed, the birds ceased to sing, and the flocks to bleat. They turned their eyes every way, and saw a being of mighty stature advancing through the valley, whom they knew to be the Genius of Distribution. In one hand he held the sheaves of plenty, and in the other the sabre of destruction. The shepherds stood trembling, and would have retired before him; but he called to them with a voice gentle as the evening breeze. "Fly not from your benefactor, children of the dust! I am come to offer you gifts, which only your own folly can make vain—you here pray for water, and water I will bestow: let me know with how much you will be satisfied: speak not rashly; consider that of whatever can be enjoyed by the body, excess is no less dangerous than scarcity. When you remember the pain of thirst, do not forget the pain of suffocation. Now Hamet tell me your request."

"O being, kind and beneficent," says Hamet, "let thine eye pardon my confusion. I entreat a little brook, which in summer shall never be dry, and in winter never overflow." "It is granted," replies the genius; and immediately he opened the ground with his sabre, and a fountain bubbling up under their feet, scattered its rills over the meadows: the flowers renewed their fragrance, the trees spread a green foliage, and the flocks and herds quenched their thirst.

Then, turning to Raschid, the Genius invited him likewise to offer his petition. "I request," says Raschid, "that thou wilt turn the Ganges through my grounds, with all his waters, and all their inhabitants. Hamet was struck with the greatness of his neighbour's sentiments, and secretly repined in his heart that he had not made the same petition before him, when the genius spoke, "Rash man, be not so insatiate; remember! to thee that is nothing which thou can'st not use: and how are thy wants greater than the wants of Hamet?" Raschid repeated his desire, and pleased himself with the mean appearance that Hamet would make in the presence of the proprietor of the Ganges. The genius then retired towards the river, and the two shepherds stood waiting the event. As Raschid was looking with contempt upon his neighbour, on a sudden was heard the roar of torrents, and they found by the mighty stream that the mounds of the Ganges were broken. The flood rolled forward into the lands of Raschid, his plantations were torn up, his flocks overwhelmed, he was swept away before it, and a crocodile devoured him.—JOHNSON.

### ROBINSON CRUSOE.

And now resolving to see the circumference of my little kingdom, I victualled my ship for the voyage, putting in two dozen of my barley-bread loaves, an earthen pot full of parched rice, a little bottle of rum, half a goat, powder and shot, and two coats. It was the 6th of November, in the 6th year of my captivity, that I set out on this voyage, and which was much longer than I expected, being obliged to put farther out, on account of the rocks. And indeed, so much did these rocks surprise me, that I was for putting back, fearing that if I ventured farther it would be out of my power to return. In this uncertainty I came to anchor just on shore, to which I waded with my gun on my shoulder, and then climbing a hill, which overlooked that point, I saw the full extent of it, and resolved to run all hazards. That night it grew so calm that I ventured out; and here I may be a monument to all rash and ignorant pilots; for I was no sooner come to the point, and not above a boat's length from shore, but I was got into deep water, with a current like a mill, which drove my boat along so violently, that it was impossible for me to keep near the edge of it, but forced me more and more out from the eddy to the left of me; and all I could do with my paddles was useless, there being no wind to help me.

Who can conceive the present anguish of my mind at this calamity? With longing eyes did I look upon my little kingdom, and thought the island the pleasantest place in the universe, "Happy, thrice happy desert," said I. "Shall I never see thee more? wretched creature! whither am I going? why did I murmur at my lonesome condition, when now I would give the whole world to be thither again?" While I was thus complaining, I found myself driven about two leagues into the sea; however, I laboured till my strength was far spent, to keep my boat as far north as possible. About noon, I perceived a little breeze of wind spring up, which overjoyed my heart; and I was still more elated, when in about half an hour, it blew a gentle fine gale. I set up my mast again, spread my sail, and stood away northward as much as I could, to get rid of the current. And no sooner did the boat begin to move, but I perceived by the clearness of the water, a change of the current was near. About 4 o'clock in the afternoon, I reached within a league of the island, and within an hour came within a mile of the shore, where I soon landed, to my unspeakable comfort; and after an humble prostration, thanking God for my deliverance, with resolution to lay all thoughts of escaping aside, I brought my boat safe to a little cove, and laid down to take a welcome repose.—DEFOE.

### THE JACKAL AND THE CAMEL.

There once lived a Camel and a Jackal who were great friends. One day the Jackal said to the Camel, "I know that there is a fine field of sugar-cane on the other side of the river. If you will take me across, I will show you the place; this plan will suit me as well as you. You will enjoy eating the sugar-cane, and I am sure to find many crabs, bones, and bits of fish by the river side, on which to make a good dinner."

The Camel consented, and swam across the river, taking the Jackal, who could not swim, on his back. When they reached the other side, the Camel went to eat the sugar-cane, and the Jackal ran up and down the river bank devouring all the crabs, bits of fish, and bones he could find.

But being so much smaller an animal, he had made an excellent meal before the Camel had eaten more than two or three mouthsful; and no sooner had he finished his dinner, than he ran round and round the sugar-cane field, yelping and howling with all his might.

The villagers heard him, and thought, "There is a jackal among the sugar-canes, he will be scratching holes in the ground, and spoiling the roots of the plants." And they all went down to the place to drive him away. But when they got there, they found to their surprise not only a Jackal, but a Camel who was eating the sugar-cane! This made them very angry, and they caught the poor

Camel, and drove him from the field, and beat him, until he was nearly dead.

When they had gone, the Jackal said to the Camel, "We had better go home." And the Camel said, "Very well, then jump upon my back as you did before."

So the Jackal jumped upon the Camel's back, and the Camel began to recross the river. When they had got well into the water, the Camel said, "This is a pretty way in which you have treated me, friend Jackal. No sooner had you finished your own dinner, than you must go yelping about the place loud enough to arouse the whole village, and bringing all the villagers down to beat me, and turn me out of the field before I had eaten two mouthsful! what in the world did you make such a noise for?"

"I don't know," said the Jackal, "It is a custom I have: I always like to sing a little after dinner."

The Camel waded on through the river, till the water reached up to his knees. Then turning to the Jackal he said, "I feel very anxious to roll." "Oh, pray do not; why do you wish to do so?" asked the Jackal, "I don't know," answered the Camel, "It is a custom I have, I always like to have a little roll after dinner." So saying, he rolled over in the water, shaking the Jackal off as he did so. And the Jackal was drowned, but the Camel swam safely to shore.—FRERE'S OLD DECCAN DAYS.

## ULYSSES AND HIS DOG.

When wise Ulysses, from his native coast,
Long kept by wars, and long by tempests tos't,
Arrived at last, poor, old, disguis'd, alone,
To all his friends, and ev'n his Queen, unknown:
Chang'd as he was, with age, and toils, and cares,
Furrow'd his rev'rend face, and white his hairs,

In his own palace forc'd to ask his bread,
Scorn'd by those slaves his former bounty fed,
Forgot of all his own domestic crew;
The faithful dog alone his rightful master knew.
Unfed, unhous'd, neglected, on the clay,
Like an old servant now cashier'd he lay;
Touch'd with resentment of ungrateful man,
And longing to behold his ancient Lord again.
Him when he saw—he rose, and crawl'd to meet,
('Twas all he could), and fawn'd, and kiss'd his feet,
Seiz'd with dumb joy—then falling by his side,
Own'd his returning Lord, look'd up, and died!—
POPE.

### FABLE—THE LARK AND HER YOUNG ONES.

A lark, who had young ones in a field of corn which was almost ripe, was under some fear in case the reapers should come and reap it before her young brood was fledged, and able to remove from the place. Wherefore, upon flying abroad to look for food, she left this charge with them: that they should take notice of what they heard talked of in her absence, and tell her of it when she came back again. When she was gone, they heard the owner of the corn call to his son. "Well," says he, "I think this corn is ripe enough, I would have you go early to-morrow, and desire our friends and neighbours to come and help us to reap it." When the old lark came home, the young ones fell a quivering and chirping, begging her to remove them as fast as she could. The mother bid them be easy, for, says she, "if the owner depends upon his friends and neighbours, I am pretty sure the corn will not be reaped to-morrow." Next day she went out again upon the same occasion, and left the same orders with them as before. The owner came and staid, expecting those he had sent to; but the sun grew hot, and nothing was done, for not a soul came to help him. "Then," says he to his son, "I perceive these friends of ours are not to be depended upon, so that you must even go to your uncles and cousins and tell them I desire that they would be here betimes to-morrow morning to help us to reap." Well, this the young ones in a great fright reported also to their mother. "If that be all," says she, "do not be frightened, children, for kindred and relations do not use to be so very forward to serve one another; but take particular notice what you hear said the next time, and be sure you let me know it." She went abroad the next day as usual, and the owner, finding his relations as slack as the rest of his neighbours, said to his son, "Hark ye, George, do you get a couple of good sickles ready against to-morrow morning, and we will even reap the corn ourselves." When the young ones told their mother this, "Then," says she, "we must be gone indeed; for when a man undertakes to do his business himself, it is not so likely he will be disappointed." So she removed her young ones immediately, and the corn was reaped the next day by the good man and his son.—ÆSOP'S FABLES.

THE POOR COBBLER AND THE FAIRIES.

Many years ago in a small Cornish village there dwelt a poor, honest, hard-working cobbler, who barely managed to earn sufficient to support himself and his wife. Day by day matters became worse and worse, till at length he had only sufficient leather left in his shop to make a solitary pair of boots. So, cutting them out all ready to stitch them next morning, he retired to bed. Imagine his surprise when he went to his shop to find the shoes all finished and complete; indeed, so well were they sewn, that a customer happening to look in, was so pleased with them, that he at once gave the cobbler a handsome sum for them; this enabled the poor man to buy leather for two more pairs of boots. So, cutting them out, he left them ready as before for the morning: again he found them, on awaking, ready to hand. This continued morning after morning. Matters now began to prosper with the cobbler, so one day he proposed to his wife to watch and see who the generous benefactor might be, who thus day by day befriended him. They therefore next night secreted themselves behind a curtain, in anxious expectation as to what they would see. At midnight two little fairy dwarfs took their seat upon the shoemaker's bench, and at once set to work completing the shoes which they found ready cut. As soon as they had finished their task, they hurried away, leaving the cobbler and his wife wrapt in astonishment.

Next day the woman said to her husband, "These dear little creatures, who have been so kind to us, do not appear to have any clothing. Suppose I make each of them a suit of clothes, and you stitch them some shoes. Delighted with the idea of befriending their benefactors, the good man and his spouse immediately set to work and got the things ready; they then as before placed them on the bench, and secreted themselves to see what the little fairies would do. At the usual time the tiny creatures made their appearance, and much pleased at the garments prepared for them, they at once arrayed themselves in their new attire, and merrily danced about with glee: till, at length, away they bounded out of the cobbler's sight.

From that time forward, says the legend, everything prospered with him as long as he lived.—CORNISH FAIRY TALE.

## ANECDOTE OF M. BERRYER.

M. Berryer, who was one of the greatest and most eloquent French statesmen of the present century, in his youth was very lazy. His master had great trouble in making him submit to school discipline; he refused to exercise that memory which afterwards became so remarkable. The under-masters quite despaired of him, and went one day to tell the head-master that this boy would never do anything, and that they could not make anything of him. This gentleman, who was a man of sense, argued differently of Berryer. He sent for him into his study, and said to him, "My boy, work is disagreeable to you, and you think that happiness consists in doing nothing. Well, come into my study; you can look at me while I am at work—that will not fatigue you, and you will do nothing—but let us well understand each other; nothing of any kind, remember."

The boy was delighted. Here he was in the kind master's study, who went on working, taking no more notice of him than if he had been a piece of furniture in the room. The first hour passed away to the great pleasure of the scholar. He triumphed in thought over the usher who had to teach him; he congratulated himself on neither having to open his dictionary, nor learn his rudiments by heart. At the end of an hour and a half, however, he had sufficiently enjoyed the delights of fancy. He put out his arm to take a book. The master stopped him at once. "My boy," he said, "you forget our agreement; you are to do nothing. To read is to do something. Enjoy the permission I have given you—do nothing."

The boy began to discover that the pleasure of doing nothing soon became monotonous. He hazarded some questions; the master did not reply. Then, when he had come to the end of the page he was writing, he said, "My boy, each has his taste; you have that of doing nothing, I have that of working. I do not trouble you in your repose, so do not disturb me in my work."

Young Berryer could scarcely help saying that it would be difficult for him to find happiness much longer in such patience. At the end of three hours the master got up, and went to take a walk under the shade of the trees in the park. "Good!" said the boy to himself, "now I am relieved from my imprisonment. I can amuse myself now." As soon as he came into the garden he wished to leave his master, and go and mingle with his schoolfellows, who were having a merry game. The master held him by the arm. "My boy, you are not thinking of our agreement; playing is doing something. Remain by my side, we will walk up and down this avenue, or you can sit down if you like better."

Honest and excellent master! a man of sense and talent, to whom, perhaps, the world owes the great Berryer. Instead of repeating to him how delightful work was, he made him love it by making him feel how insupportable was a life of idleness.—ANON.

### EDUCATION IN INDIA.

We have to educate a people who cannot at present be educated by the means of their mother-tongue. We must teach them some foreign language; the claims of our own language it is hardly necessary to recapitulate. It stands pre-eminent among the languages of the West. It abounds with works of imagination, not inferior to the noblest which Greece has bequeathed to us; with models of every species of eloquence; with historical compositions, which, considered merely as narratives, have seldom been surpassed, and which, considered as vehicles of general and political instruction, have never been equalled; with just and lively representations of human life and human nature; with the most profound speculations on metaphysics, morals, government, jurisprudence, and trade; with full and correct information respecting every experimental science which tends to preserve the wealth, to increase the comfort, or to expand the intellect of man. Whoever knows that language has ready access to all the vast intellectual wealth which all the wisest nations of the earth have created and hoarded in the course of ninety generations. It may safely be said, that the literature now extant in that language is of far greater value than all the literature which three hundred years ago was extant in all the languages of the world together. Nor is this all. In India, English is the language spoken by the ruling class. In is spoken by the higher class of natives at the seats of government. It is likely to become the language of commerce throughout the seas of the East. It is the language of two great European communities which are rising, the one in the south of Africa, the other in Australasia; communities which are every year becoming more important and more closely connected with our Indian empire. Whether we look at the intrinsic value of our literature, or at the particular situation of this country (India) we shall see the strongest reason to think that, of all foreign tongues, the English tongue is that which would be the most useful to our native subjects.—MACAULAY.

### LIVINGSTONE AND THE LION.

It is well known that if one in a troop of lions is killed, the others take the hint and leave that part of the country. So the next time the herds were attacked I went with the people, in order to encourage them to rid themselves of the annoyance by destroying one of the marauders. We found the lions on a small hill about a quarter of a mile in length, and covered with trees. . . . A circle of men was formed round it, and they gradually closed up, ascending pretty near to each other. Being down below on the plain with a native schoolmaster, named Mebálme, a most excellent man, I saw one of the lions sitting on a piece of rock within the now closed circle of men, Mebálme fired at him before I could, and the ball struck the rock on which the animal was sitting. He bit at the spot struck, as a dog does at a stick or stone thrown at him; then leaping away, broke through the opening circle and escaped unhurt. The men were afraid to attack him, perhaps on account of their belief in witchcraft. When the circle was reformed, we saw two lions in it, but we were afraid to fire, lest we should strike the men, and they allowed the beasts to burst through also. If they had acted according to the custom of the country, they would have speared the lions in their attempt to get out. . . . . Seeing we could not get them to kill one of the lions, we bent our footsteps towards the village; in going round the end of the hill, however, I saw one of the beasts sitting on a piece of rock as before, but this time he had a little bush in front. Being about thirty yards off, I took a good aim at his body through the bush, and fired both barrels into it. The men then called out, "He is shot, he is shot!" Others cried, "He has been shot by another man too; let us go to him!" I did not see anyone else shoot at him, but I saw the lion's tail erected in anger behind the bush, and turning to the people said, "Stop a little till I load again." When in the act of ramming down the bullets I heard a shout. Starting and looking half round, I saw the lion just in the act of springing upon me. I was upon a little height; he caught my shoulder as he sprang, and we both came to the ground below together. Growling horribly close to my ear, he shook me as a dog does a rat. The shock produced a stupor similar to that which seems to be felt by a mouse after the first shake of the cat. It caused a sort of dreaminess, in which there was no sense of pain or feeling of terror, though full consciousness of all that was happening. This singular condition was not the result of any mental process. The shake annihilated fear, and allowed no sense of horror in looking round at the beast. This peculiar state is probably produced in all animals killed by beasts of prey; and if so, is a merciful provision by the Creator for lessening the pain of death. Turning round to relieve myself of the weight, as he had one paw on the back of my head, I saw his eyes directed to my servant Mebálme, who was trying to shoot him at a distance of ten or fifteen yards. His gun missed fire in both barrels; the lion immediately left me, and attacking him bit his thigh. Another man, whose life I had saved before, after he had been tossed by a buffalo, attempted to spear the lion while he was biting Mebálme. Him he left, and caught this man by the shoulder, but at that moment the bullets he had received took effect, and he fell down dead. The whole was the work of a few moments, and must have been his paroxysm of dying rage. Besides crunching the bone into splinters, he left eleven wounds on the upper part of my arm.—LIVINGSTONE.

### THE GOLDSMITH AND THE SOLDIER.

In a certain city there lived a very wealthy goldsmith, with whom a soldier had formed a friendship, which being heartfelt on his part, he thought it also sincere on the part of the goldsmith. It so happened that the said soldier once found somewhere a bag full of gold. Filled with delight, he opened it, and on counting the pieces of money found them to amount to 250 in all. Forthwith he repaired to his friend the goldsmith in great glee, and said to him, "I have been most lucky to find, without any trouble or toil, such a sum of gold on the road." Ultimately he trusted the bag and its contents to the goldsmith, saying to him, "Brother, allow me to deposit it with you, and when I require it, I will get it from you again." Well, some time after, the soldier asked the goldsmith for his bag, upon which the fellow had the impudence to say to him, "Is this the reason forsooth that you made friendship with me, that you might fasten a calumny upon me, and make me out a thief? When did you give me a bag? You tell a falsehood! A fine affair indeed! Be off with you, and fasten your accusation on some man of wealth, and by that means you may get something to your liking. Little did I think that you would become my enemy. Conjoining truth with falsehood you now want to rob me of my property. It reminds one of the well-known proverb, 'Instead of the thief they punish the judge; the honest man dies weeping before the rogue.'"

The upshot was that the poor soldier had no help for it but to go to the judge and make a complaint, which he accordingly did, recounting to him all the circumstances most minutely. The judge then asked him, "Have you any witnesses to the charge?" He replied, "No, your worship, I have no witnesses." The judge shrewdly conjectured that there would be no wonder if the goldsmith had acted dishonestly as stated. Acting on this conjecture, the judge sent for the goldsmith and his wife, but much as he tried by coaxing and persuasion, to get them to confess, they persisted in denying the charge. At last the judge said to them, "I know for certain that you have made off with the bag, so, until you return it, I am determined I will not release you." Having thus said he went home, and thereupon shut up two confidential servants in a chest which he had placed in a certain room. Then returning again into the court, he said to the goldsmith, "If you do not consent to give the man back his gold, I shall have you put to death in the morning." Having thus spoken, he shut them both up in the said room, and telling them that he would execute them next morning, he retired to his private apartments. After midnight, the wife said to her husband, "If you really have taken the man's bag, then tell me where you have concealed it, otherwise my life, as well as the bag, will be lost. The judge will never let us off without getting the bag." The goldsmith thereupon told her that it was buried in a certain spot close by his bedstead. The two men in the box overheard this disclosure, and in the morning, when the judge sent for all four persons into his Court, and asked the two men what the other two individuals had said one to another during the night, they swore that they had heard to the above effect. The judge, therefore, sent and got the bag from the place indicated, gave it to the soldier, and hanged the goldsmith.—TALES OF A PARROT.

FABLE—THE TOWN MOUSE AND THE COUNTRY MOUSE.

An honest, plain, sensible country mouse, is said to have entertained at his hole, one day, a fine mouse of the town. Having formerly been play fellows together, they were old acquaintances, which served as an apology for the visit. However, as master of the house, he thought himself obliged to do the honours of it, in all respects, and to make as great a stranger of his guest as he possibly could. In order to do this, he set before him a dish of delicate meat cooked with green peas, and a pan of fine oatmeal, as well as some pieces of cheese; and to crown all, the remnant of a charming ripe apple. In good manners, he forebore to eat any himself, lest the stranger should not have enough; but, that he might seem to bear the other company, sat and nibbled a piece of straw very busily. At length the Town mouse said to his friend, "How can you bear to live in this nasty, dirty, melancholy hole here, with nothing but woods, meadows, and mountains, and rivulets about you? Do not you prefer the conversation of the world to the chirping of birds, and the splendour of a court to the sad aspect of an uncultivated desert? Come, take my word for it, you will find it a change for the better. Never stand considering, but away this moment. Remember we are not immortal, and therefore have no time to lose. Make sure of to-day, and spend it as agreeably as you can, you know not what may happen to-morrow." In short, these, and such like arguments prevailed, and his country acquaintance was resolved to go to town that night. So they both set out upon their journey together, proposing to sneak in after the close of the evening. They did so; and about midnight, made their entry into a certain great house, where there had been an extraordinary entertainment the day before; and several delicate morsels, which some of the servants purloined, were hid under the seat of a window; the country guest was immediately placed in the midst of a rich Persian carpet; and now it was the courtier's turn to entertain, who, indeed, acquitted himself in that capacity with the utmost readiness and address, changing the dishes most elegantly, and tasting everything previous to offering it to his guest, who sat enjoying himself to the utmost, when, on a sudden, a noise of somebody opening the door made them start from their seats, and run away in confusion about the dining room. Our country friend, in particular, was ready to die with fear at the barking of a huge mastiff or two, which opened their throats just about the same time, and made the whole house echo. At last, recovering himself, "Well, says he, if this be your town-life, much good may you do with it, give me my poor quiet hole again, with my homely, but comfortable fare."—ÆSOP'S FABLES.

### THE BALD EAGLE.

The celebrated cataract of Niagara is a noted place of resort for the bald eagle, as well on account of the fish procured there, as for the numerous carcases of deer, bears, and various other animals that, in their attempts to cross the river above the falls, have been dragged into the current, and precipitated down that tremendous gulf, where, among the rocks that bound the rapids below, they furnish a rich repast for the vulture, the raven, and the bald eagle, the subject of the present account. Formed by nature for braving the severest cold, feeding equally on the produce of the sea and of the land, possessing powers of flight capable of outstripping even the tempests themselves, unawed by anything but man, and, from the ethereal heights to which he soars, looking abroad at one glance on an immeasurable expanse of forests, fields, lakes, and ocean below him, he appears indifferent to the little inconveniences of change of seasons, as in a few minutes he can pass from summer to winter, from the lower to the higher regions of the atmosphere, the abode of eternal cold, and from thence descend at will to the torrid * or the arctic * regions of the earth.

* Hot and cold.

In procuring his food, he displays, in a very singular manner, the genius and energy of his character, which is fierce, contemplative, daring, and tyrannical; attributes not exerted save on particular occasions, but when put forth, overpowering all opposition. Elevated on the high, dead limb of some gigantic tree that commands a wide view of the neighbouring shore and ocean, he seems calmly to contemplate the motions of the various feathered tribes that pursue their busy avocations below; the snow-white gulls slowly winnowing the air; the busy quails coursing o'er the sands; trains of ducks streaming over the surface; silent and watchful cranes intent and wading; clamorous crows; and all the winged multitudes that subsist by the bounty of this vast liquid magazine of nature. High over all these, hovers one whose action instantly arrests his whole attention. By his wide curvature of wing, and sudden suspension in air, he knows him to be the fish-hawk, settling over some devoted victim of the deep. His eye kindles at the sight, and balancing himself with half-opened wings on the branch, he watches the result. Down, rapid as an arrow from heaven, descends the distant object of his attention, the roar of its wings reaching the ear as it disappears in the deep, making the surges foam around. At this moment the eager looks of the eagle are all ardour; and, levelling his neck for flight, he sees the fish-hawk once more emerge, struggling with his prey, and mounting in the air with screams of exultation. These are the signal for our hero, who, launching into the air, instantly gives chase, and soon gains on the fish-hawk; each exerts his utmost to mount above the other, displaying the most elegant and sublime aerial evolutions. The unencumbered eagle rapidly advances, and, is just on the point of reaching his opponent, when, with a sudden scream, probably of despair and honest execration, the latter drops his fish; the eagle, poising himself for a moment, as if to take a more certain aim, descends like a whirlwind, snatches it in his grasp ere it reaches the water, and bears his ill-gotten booty silently away to the woods.—ALEX. WILSON.

### THE DOG AND THE CRANE.

A mongrel dog, a surly elf,
Who ne'er loved aught except himself,
As once, half chew'd, he gorged his prey,
He found a bone obstruct the way;
Then to the crane, in feeble tone,
He made the dire disaster known;
Adding (to make assurance sure)
That vast rewards should pay the cure.
The crane at once complied, and drew
The latent splinter forth to view.
The savage, freed from pain and fear,
Beheld his friend with scornful sneer;
"What! now, no doubt, you want your hire,
Thou mercenary fool—retire,"
(The graceless ruffian taunting said),
"And thank me that you wear your head."
The generous bird reply disdained,
And spurn'd the ground the wretch profaned,
Look'd up with yet unanger'd eye,
And clapp'd her wings, and sought the sky.
The dog meantime, with inward pain,
Her careless air and just disdain
Beheld: he cursed the glorious sight
With all the rage of thwarted spite;
The keen remorse assail'd him sore,
And gave a pang unfelt before;

With persevering feet, behind
Him justice traced, though lame and blind;
When next he tasted living food
He found his late mischance renew'd,
Another bone his throat retains,
And doubles all his former pains:
At once a thousand thoughts combined,
Like lightning flash'd upon his mind;
They stung, they blasted, as they came,
With conscious guilt, reproach, and shame:
Cursed dog—to guile more cursed a prey,
He groan'd—as stretch'd on earth he lay.
A bird who heard him thus complain,
Flew straight and told her friend the crane,
She hastes th' expiring wretch to find,
Who thus display'd his rankling mind:
"Comest thou to blast my dying ear?
Why! take thy wish,—I'm bound to bear
Reproach and insult, storm and hate;
Come all, and urge the hand of fate."
Conscious of worth superior, smiled
The crane, and thus his fears beguiled:
"Learn better thoughts—look up and trace
The marks of mercy in my face;
I court the nobler task to show
That virtue still resides below;
To make thy stubborn soul believe
There still are those who, wrong'd relieve;
Thy life again I come to give,
And more, a pattern how to live."
The cur, who, still of guile afraid,
Knew death at hand without her aid,
Since now his death could be but sure,

He thought it best to risk a cure.
Again the crane exerts her art,
The splinter leaves the wounded part:
The dog, astonish'd, dumb with awe,
The exalted bounty felt and saw;
Grovelling in dust, he durst not meet
Her eye, and crawl'd and lick'd her feet;
Contempt itself and just disdain
Had given but half the shame and pain.
The crane with mildness raised her head,
Whilst thus the vanquish'd sinner said;
" Oh! let me find some happy way
One mite of my vast debt to pay;
Make me henceforth your faithful slave,
And deign to use the life you gave;
So shall I dare once more to rise,
Once more to meet those friendly eyes."
The bird replied, " you owe me nought;
I've gained the sole reward I sought,
The joy, the glory to impart
The virtue that first warm'd the heart;
To heaven thy adoration pay,
Its servant I, who, pleased, obey:
Be virtuous then, and blessed " she said,
Exulting clapp'd her wings, and fled.
The dog arose, resolved no more
A thief to prowl the forest o'er,
Was ever at his master's side,
A faithful servant till he died.

—NORTHCOTE'S FABLES.

### THE CHARGE OF THE LIGHT BRIGADE.

At ten minutes past eleven our light cavalry brigade

advanced. The whole brigade scarcely made one effective regiment, according to the numbers of continental armies, and yet it was more than we could spare. As they rushed towards the front, the Russians opened on them from the guns in the redoubt on the right with volleys of musketry and rifles. They swept proudly past, glittering in the morning sun in all the pride and splendour of war. We could scarcely believe the evidence of our senses! Surely that handful of men are not going to charge an army in position! Alas! it was but too true! Their desperate valour knew no bounds, and far indeed was it removed from its so-called better part—discretion. They advanced in two lines, quickening their pace as they closed towards the enemy. A more fearful spectacle was never witnessed than by those who beheld these heroes rush into the arms of death.

At the distance of 1,200 yards the whole line of the enemy belched forth from thirty iron mouths a flood of smoke and flame, through which hissed the deadly balls. Their flight was marked by gaps in our ranks, by dead men and horses, by steeds flying wounded or riderless across the plain. The first line is broken—it is joined by the second—they never halt, or check their speed an instant—with diminished ranks, thinned by those thirty guns, which the Russians had laid with the most deadly accuracy—with a halo of flashing steel above their heads—and with a cheer which was many a noble fellow's death-cry, they flew into the smoke of the batteries; but ere they were lost from view, the plain was strewed with their bodies, and with the carcases of horses. They were exposed to an oblique fire from the batteries on the hills on both sides, as well as to a direct fire of musketry. Through the clouds of smoke we could see their sabres flashing as they rode up to the guns and dashed between them, cutting down the gunners as they stood. We saw them riding through the guns, as I have said; to our delight we saw them returning after breaking through a column of Russian infantry, and scattering them like chaff, when the flank fire of the battery on the hill swept them down, scattered and broken as they were. Wounded men and dismounted troopers flying towards us told the sad tale. Demigods conld not have done what they had failed to do. At the very moment when they were about to retreat, an enormous mass of Lancers was hurled on their flank. Colonel Shewell, of the 8th Hussars, saw the danger, and rode his few men straight at them, cutting his way through with fearful loss. The other regiments turned, and engaged in a desperate encounter. With courage too great almost for credence, they were breaking their way through the columns which enveloped them, when there took place an act of atrocity without parallel in the modern warfare of civilised nations. The Russian gunners, when the storm of cavalry passed, returned to their guns. They saw their own cavalry mingled with the troopers who had just ridden over them; and, to the eternal disgrace of the Russian name, the miscreants poured a murderous volley on the mass of struggling men and horses, mingling friend and foe in one common ruin. It was as much as our heavy cavalry brigade could do to cover the retreat of the miserable remnants of the band of heroes as they returned to the place they had so lately quitted. At thirty-five minutes past eleven not a British soldier, except the dead and dying, was left in front of these guns.—RUSSELL.

### THE MONKEY AND THE CHILD.

In the year 1818 a handsome vessel that sailed between Whitehaven and Kingston, Jamaica, started on her homeward voyage, and among other passengers was a lady, the mother of an infant only a few weeks old.

When the weather permitted, the mother took regular exercise on deck, sometimes with the infant in her arms, but oftener at a moment when it had been hushed to sleep by the motion of the ship, the rushing of the waters, and the whisperings of the breeze.

In August the weather became remarkably fine; and one beautiful afternoon, when the vessel was majestically speeding along, the captain perceived a distant sail—a sight that is always welcome at sea, and which, amidst the vast solitudes of the Atlantic, may be compared to the meeting of pilgrims in a desert.

The discovery attracted the attention of all on board, and after the captain had gratified his curiosity, he politely offered his glass to the lady alluded to, that she might obtain a clear view of an object which the naked eye was unable to distinguish from the fleecy clouds which overspread the horizon.

At this moment she had the baby in her arms, but she immediately wrapped her shawl about it; and placed it on the sofa on which she had been sitting. The captain assisted her to steady the glass, but scarcely had she applied her eye to it than the helmsman cried, in a voice trembling with emotion, "See what that mischievous monkey has done!"

The mother's feelings may be imagined, when, on instantly turning round, she saw that a large, strong, and active monkey, which was on board the vessel, had grasped the infant firmly with one arm, and with the other was nimbly climbing the shrouds, evidently intent on reaching the very top of the mainmast. One look was sufficient for the terrified mother, and that look had well-nigh been her last. Though she attempted to speak, the words died away on her lips, or were rendered inarticulate by her sobs and groans, and had it not been for the prompt assistance of those around, she would have fallen on the deck, where she was soon after laid, to all appearance a corpse.

At this crisis the captain was sore distressed. When he looked at the mother, speechless, motionless, and deadly pale, he almost fancied that life had fled: and when he thought of the child borne far aloft by so strange a nurse, he dreaded every moment that the capricious monkey would have become tired of its toy, and either dash it on the deck or drop it in the ocean. Often as he had crossed the wide Atlantic, braved its perils and borne the terrors of the winter's storm, never, amidst all the chances and changes of a seaman's life, had his feelings been exposed to so severe a trial. It is true the sailors could climb as well as the monkey, but any attempt to capture it was dangerous, for the moment they endeavoured to put a foot on the shrouds, the captain feared that it would drop the child and endeavour to escape by leaping from one mast to another.

In the meantime the infant was heard to cry; and though many supposed from this that it was suffering pain, their fears on this point were speedily dissipated, when they observed the monkey imitating exactly the motions of a nurse, by dandling, soothing, and caressing the child, and even endeavouring to hush it to sleep.

Many a plan had been tried to lure the culprit from the mast-head, but, finding all fail, the captain, as a last resort, ordered every man to conceal himself below. The order was promptly obeyed, and he now took a seat where he could see without being seen. To his indescribable relief, the monkey, on finding that the coast was clear, cautiously descended from the mast-head, and replaced the infant on the sofa from which it was taken, cold, fretful, and perhaps frightened, but in every other respect free from injury. The captain had now a most grateful task to perform, and the babe was immediately restored to its mother's arms.—CASSELL'S NATURAL HISTORY.

### THE ANT.

Turn on the prudent ant thy heedful eyes,
Observe her labours, sluggard, and be wise;
No stern command, no monitory voice,
Prescribes her duties, or directs her choice;
Yet, timely provident, she hastes away,
To snatch the blessings of the plenteous day;
When fruitful summer loads the teeming plain,
She crops the harvest, and she stores the grain.
How long shall sloth usurp thy useless hours,
Unnerve thy vigour, and enchain thy powers;
While artful shades thy downy couch enclose,
And soft solicitation courts repose?
Amidst the drowsy charms of dull delight,
Year chases year with unremitted flight,
Till Want, now following, fraudulent and slow,
Shall spring to seize thee like an ambush'd foe.
—JOHNSON.

### DEATH OF THE SON OF KING HENRY I.

The fleet destined for the return of the royal party from Normandy to England was lying in the port of Harfleur, in the month of December, 1120, and all things were ready for the reception of the voyagers. They were on the point of weighing anchor, when a Norman mariner, called Fitz-Stephen, approaching King Henry I. and presenting him with a piece of gold, thus addressed him:—

"Etienne, son of Herard, my father, all his life, followed thy father on the sea! he steered the vessel in which thy father sailed to the conquest of England. I ask of thee that thou wouldst grant me the like honour. I have a ship, called La Blanche Nef, in readiness for thee; sail in her as thy father did in the ship of my father."

The King replied that it was too late to change the vessel destined for his own conveyance, but that in consideration of the request of a son of Etienne, the young prince and all the treasure should be confided to his safe conduct. This compromise being accepted, the King embarked and reached England in safety. But Prince William spent several hours on deck, feasting and dancing with his gay and thoughtless companions, before he would permit the anchor of the Blanche Nef to be lifted.

The vessel was manned by fifty skilful rowers; the son of Etienne was at the helm, and they held their course rapidly under a clear moon, coasting along Normandy, before reaching the open sea. The rowers, stimulated by the wine, with which in the riot of the moment they had been too plentifully supplied, resolved on attempting to overtake the vessel of the king; but, too eager to accomplish this, they incautiously entangled themselves among the rocks by which that dangerous coast is protected. The hand of the helmsman proved untrue, and, amidst the shouts and merriment of her disorderly company, the white ship struck with all the velocity of her course, and immediately began to fill.

Prince William was instantly lowered into a boat, and might with ease have reached the shore, but the screams of his sister Adela recalled him to her aid; numbers rushed into the small boat as she once more approached the sinking bark, and she was instantly swamped, all within perishing immediately! The ship itself went down very soon after, and all on board—to the number of three hundred persons, among whom were one hundred and forty of the Norman nobility, with eighteen noble ladies—were buried in the waves.

The despairing cry of the sufferers was heard from the other vessels, already far at sea, but no one dared even to suspect the extent of the mischief that had happened, and all proceeded quietly on their course. But of all the gay crowds that had so joyously embarked, two persons only saved themselves by clinging to a yard. Fitz-Stephen sunk with the rest, but rising to the surface, and well able to swim, he made for these men, calling out, "The Prince! what has become of the Prince?" "We have seen no more of him, nor of his brother, nor of his sister, nor of any of their companions," was the mournful reply.

"Woe is me," exclaimed the despairing captain; he too might have held by the spar, but hearing the tidings that had been given him, he refused all further effort, and voluntarily sank beneath the waves.

The night was extremely cold, and the weaker of the two survivors, benumbed and worn out by his sufferings, lost his grasp of the spar, and sank while in the act of expressing a hope that his companion might hold out better, and this prayer was heard. Berauld, the last survivor, and among the humblest of all who had entered that ill-fated bark, was wrapped in the sheep skin doublet of the Norman peasant; this saved him from expiring of cold. He continued to support himself on the surface until morning, when he was picked up by a fishing-boat, and from his lips the details given above were gained.

It is said that for many days after the fatal intelligence had reached England, there was no one who could be prevailed on to communicate the terrible secret to the king; naturally alarmed by his son's delay, he yet persisted in maintaining that the prince had chosen to put in at some distant port; nor could the melancholy looks of those around him induce the unhappy father to turn his thoughts towards the dreadful truth. At length a boy was instructed to throw himself weeping at the king's feet, and by a series of questions the wretched father at length elicited the lamentable fate of his children. But all these precautions to break the matter gradually, could not ward off the anguish of the blow. Henry fainted when his loss became apparent, and was never afterwards seen to smile.—STORIES FROM ENGLISH HISTORY, (HALL).

### AFRICAN MONKEYS ON MARCH.

About half way across a plain we were traversing, runs a beautiful stream, which coming down from the hills to the west of Mardemas, crosses the road, forming many pretty cascades and eddies with the large stones that occupy its bed; and, dashing onward, falls into a deep ravine, or crack, in the plain, where at length it joins the Mareb. On the north side of the stream are two plantations, both growing so regularly and the different trees so well distributed for effect of mass and colour, that you might easily deceive yourself into the idea of the whole scene being carefully arranged by some gardener of exquisite taste. Had it really been so, he could not have chosen a prettier spot, nor one where his labour would have been more profitably bestowed, than at the half-way halt on the wide and desolate plain we were crossing. From the vicinity of water the grass round these plantations was a bright green, unlike the dry herbage of the plain, and this formed no slight addition to its merits, both in the eyes of the mules and their masters.

The ravine down which the brook fell was well wooded, and the trees were filled with beautiful little monkeys. I followed a troop of these for a long time, while the porters and servants were resting, merely for the pleasure of watching their movements. If you go tolerably carefully towards them, they will allow you to approach very near, and you will be much amused with their proceedings, which differ little from those of the large monkeys. You may see them quarrelling, making love, mothers taking care of their children, combing their hair, nursing and suckling them, and the passions, jealousy, anger, and love, as distinctly marked as in men.

The monkeys have their chiefs, whom they obey implicitly, and they practise a regular system of warfare. These monkey forays are managed with the utmost regularity and precaution. A tribe, coming down to feed from their haunt on the mountain, brings with it all its members, male and female, old and young. Some, the elders of the tribe, distinguishable by the quantity of hair covering their shoulders like a lion's, take the lead, looking over each precipice before they descend, and climbing cautiously to the top of every rock or stone, which may afford them a better view of the road before them. Others have their posts as scouts on the flank or rear; and all fulfil their duties with the utmost vigilance, calling out at times, apparently to keep order among the mass which forms the main body, or to give notice of any real or imagined danger. Their tones of voice on these occasions are so distinctly varied, that a person much accustomed to watch their movements will at length fancy that he can understand their signals.

The main body is composed of females, inexperienced males, and young people of the tribe. Those of the females who have small children carry them on their backs. Unlike the dignified march of the leaders, the rabble go along in a most disorderly manner, trotting on and chattering, without taking the least heed of anything, apparently confiding in the vigilance of their scouts. Here a few of the youth linger behind to pick the berries off some tree, but not long, for the advancing rear-guard forces them to regain their places. There a matron pauses for a moment to suckle her offspring; and, not to lose time, dresses its hair while it is taking its meal. Another younger lady, probably excited by jealousy or by some sneering look or word, pulls an ugly mouth at her neighbour, and then uttering a shrill cry highly expressive of rage, vindictively snatches at her rivals leg or tail. This provokes a retort, and a most unladylike quarrel ensues, till a loud bark from one of the chiefs calls them to order. A single cry of alarm makes them all halt, and remain on the alert, till another bark in a different tone reassures them, and then they proceed on their march.

Arrived at the corn field, the scouts take their position on the eminences all round, while the remainder of the tribe collect provision with all expedition, filling their cheeks as full as they can hold, and placing the heads of corn under their armpits. They show equal sagacity in searching for water, discovering at once the places where it is most readily found in the sand, and then digging for it with their hands, relieving one another if the quantity of sand to be removed be considerable.—M. PARKYNS.

### CONVERSATION OF THE VULTURES.

As I was sitting, said a shepherd, within a hollow rock, and watching my sheep that fed in the valley, I heard two vultures interchangeably crying on the summit of a cliff.

Both voices were earnest and deliberate. My curiosity prevailed over the care of the flock: I climbed slowly and silently from crag to crag, concealed among the shrubs, till I found a cavity where I might sit and listen without suffering, or giving disturbance.

I soon perceived that my labour would be well repaid, for an old vulture was sitting on a naked prominence, with her young about her, whom she was instructing in the arts of a vulture's life, and preparing, by the last lecture, for their final dismission to the mountains and the skies.

"My children," said the old vulture, "you will the less want my instruction, because you have had my practice before your eyes: you have seen me snatch from the farm the household fowl; you have seen me seize the leveret in the bush, and the kid in the pasturage; you know how to fix your talons, and how to balance your flight when you are laden with your prey. But you remember the taste of more delicious food. I have often regaled you with the flesh of man." "Tell us," said the young vultures, "where man may be found, and how he may be known; his flesh is surely the natural food of a vulture. Why have you never brought a man in your talons to the nest?" "He is too bulky," said the mother: "when we find a man we can only tear away his flesh, and leave his bones upon the ground." "Since man is so big," said the young ones, "how do you kill him? You are afraid of the wolf, and of the bear, by what power are vultures superior to man? Is man more defenceless than a sheep?" "We have not the strength of man," returned the mother, "and I am sometimes in doubt whether we have the subtlety: and the vultures would seldom feast upon his flesh, had not nature, that devoted him to our uses, infused into him a strange ferocity, which I have never observed in any other being that feeds upon the earth. Two herds of men will often meet and shake the earth with noise, and fill the earth with fire. When you hear noise, and see fire, with flashes along the ground, hasten to the place with your swiftest wing, for men are surely destroying one another; you will then find the ground smoking with blood and covered with carcases, of which many are dismembered and mangled for the convenience of the vulture." "But when men have killed their prey," said the pupil, "why do they not eat it? When the wolf has killed a sheep, he suffers not the vulture to touch it till he has satisfied himself. Is not man another kind of wolf?" "Man," said the mother, "is the only beast who kills that which he does not devour, and this quality makes him so much a benefactor to our species." " If men kill our prey, and lay it in our way," said the young one, "what need shall we have of labouring for ourselves?" " Because man will sometimes," replied the mother, "remain for a long time quiet in his den. The old vulture will tell you when you are to watch his motions. When you see men in great numbers moving close together, like a flight of storks, you may conclude that they are hunting, and that you will soon revel in human blood." " But still," said the young one, " I would gladly know the reason of this mutual slaughter. I could never kill what I could not eat." "My child," said the mother, "this is a question which I cannot answer, though I am reckoned the most subtle bird of the mountain. There is in every herd, one that gives directions to the rest, and seems to be more eminently delighted with a wide carnage. What it is that entitles him to such a pre-eminence we know not; he is seldom the biggest or the swiftest, but he shows by his eagerness and diligence that he is, more than any of the others, a friend to the vulture."—JOHNSON.

### THE LION AND THE JACKALS.

Once upon a time, in a great, jungle, there lived a great lion. He was Rajah (king) of all the country round; and every day he used to leave his den, in the deepest shadow of the rocks, and roar with a loud, angry voice; and when he roared, the other animals in the jungle, who were all his subjects, got very much frightened, and ran here and there; and the lion would pounce upon them, and kill them, and eat them up for his dinner.

This went on for a long, long time, until, at last, there were no living creatures left in the jungle but two little jackals, male and female.

A very hard time of it the poor little jackals had, running this way and that to escape the terrible lion; and every day the little female jackal would say to her husband, "I am afraid he will catch us to day, do you hear how he is roaring? Oh dear, oh dear!" And he would answer her, "Never fear; I will take care of you. Let us run on a mile or two. Come, come—quick, quick, quick." And they would both run away as fast as they could.

After some time spent in this way, they found, however, one fine day, that the lion was so close upon them that they could not escape. Then the little female jackal said, "Husband, husband, I feel very frightened. The lion is so angry, he will certainly kill us at once. What can we do?" But he answered, "Cheer up, we can save ourselves yet. Come, and I will show you how we may manage it."

So what did these cunning little jackals do, but they went to the great lion's den, and when he saw them coming, he began to roar, and shake his mane, and he said, "You little wretches, come and be eaten at once! I have had no dinner for three whole days, and all that time I have been running over hill and dale to find you. Come and be eaten I say!" and he lashed his tail, and gnashed his teeth, and looked very terrible indeed. Then the male jackal, creeping quite close up to him, said, "Oh great sir, we all know you are our master, and we would have come at your bidding long ago, but indeed, sir, there is a much bigger lion even than you in this jungle, and he tried to catch hold of us and eat us up, and frightened us so much that we were obliged to run away."

"What do you mean?" growled the lion. "There is no king in this jungle but me." "Ah, sire," answered the jackal, "in truth one would think so, for you are very dreadful. Your very voice is death. But it is as we say, for we, with our own eyes, have seen one with whom you could not compete; whose equal you can no more be than we are yours; whose face is as flaming fire, his step as thunder, and his power supreme." "It is impossible!" interrupted the old lion; "but show me this rival of whom you speak so much, that I may destroy him instantly!"

Then the little jackals ran on before him until they reached a great well, and pointing down to his own reflection in the water, they said "See sire, there lives the terrible king of whom we spoke." When the lion looked down the well he became very angry, for he thought he saw another lion there. He roared and shook his great mane, and the shadow lion shook his, and looked terribly defiant. At last, overpowered with rage at the violence of his opponent, the lion sprang down to kill him at once, but no other lion was there, only the treacherous reflection, and the sides of the well were so steep that he could not get out again to punish the two jackals, who peeped over the top. After struggling for some time in the deep water, he sank to rise no more. And the little jackals threw stones down upon him from above, dancing and jumping with delight.—FRERE'S OLD DECCAN DAYS.

### TIME.

The lapse of time and rivers is the same,
Both speed their journey with a restless stream;
The silent pace, with which they steal away,
No wealth can bribe, nor prayers persuade to stay;
Alike irrevocable both when past,
And a wide ocean swallows both at last.
Though each resemble each in every part,
A difference strikes at length the musing heart;
Streams never flow in vain; where streams abound,
How laughs the land with various plenty crowned!
But time, that should enrich the nobler mind,
Neglected, leaves a weary waste behind.—COWPER.

### BUCKWHEAT.—A LEGEND.

It frequently happens, when one crosses through a field of buckwheat, after a storm, that one sees it looking quite black and singed, just as if a fierce flame had passed over it, and then a countryman says: "That comes of the lightning!" But how did it come about? Well, I will tell you what a sparrow told me, and the sparrow heard it from an aged willow, that stood in a meadow next to a field of buckwheat, and is still standing for the matter of that. It is a most venerable, large willow, though crippled, and in years; his trunk is split right through the middle, and grass and weeds are peeping out through the cleft. The tree is bending forwards and its branches are hanging down to the ground—just like long green hair.

There grew corn in the surrounding fields, not only rye

and barley, but oats—pretty oats that when ripe, look like a flight of little yellow birds sitting on a branch. The harvest was blessed with plenty, and the heavier and richer the ears of corn, the lower did they bow their heads in pious humility.

Now there was a field of buckwheat just opposite the old willow. The buckwheat did not bow its head like the rest of the corn, but boasted itself in pride and arrogance.

"I am as rich as the other ears of corn," said he: "and, moreover, I am much more sightly. My flowers are as pretty as apple-blossoms, and it is a treat to look at me and mine. Do you know of anything more beautiful than ourselves, you old willow?"

And the willow nodded his head, as much as to say: "Indeed I do!"

But the buckwheat proudly said "stupid tree! He is so old that the grass is growing on his body."

There now arose a violent storm. All the flowers of the field folded up their leaves, or bent their little heads downwards, while the storm swept over them; but the buckwheat stood erect in all its pride.

"Bow your head, as we do," said the flowers.

"There is no need of that for me," answered the buckwheat.

"Hang your head down as we do," cried the corn.

"The angel of the storm is approaching! He has wings that reach from the clouds above, down to our earth; and he will smite you before you have time to beg for mercy!"

"But I do not choose to bow down," said the buckwheat.

"Fold up you flowers, and bend your leaves," said the old willow. "Do not look at the lightning, when the cloud bursts open; even human beings dare not do that, for in the midst of lightning one may see right into heaven; but the sight strikes even human beings blind, and what would not happen to us, the produce of the earth, if we ventured on such a thing, so much humbler as we are?"

"Humbler, indeed!" said the buckwheat. "Now I happen to have a mind to take a peep into heaven." And in his pride and arrogance he dared to do so. The flashes of lightning were so awful that it seemed as if the whole world were in flames.

When this dreadful storm was quite over, both the flowers and the corn felt refreshed by the rain, as they stood in the pure, quiet air; but the buckwheat was burnt black by the lightning, and was like a dead weed upon the field.

And the old willow's branches rustled in the wind, and large drops fell from his green leaves, just as though he were shedding tears.

Then the sparrow inquired: "Why are you weeping, when all around seems blest? Look how the sun shines, and how the clouds are moving! Do you not smell the sweet perfume of flowers and bushes? Wherefore do you weep, aged willow?"

And the willow told of the buckwheat's pride, of his stubbornness, and of the punishment which is sure to follow.—ANDERSEN'S TALES.

### ANECDOTE OF BARON CUVIER.

The young tutor of the children of Count Hérig, residing in an old château, was accustomed early in the morning to inhale the fresh air of the garden into which his window opened. One morning he observed two swallows building a nest in the outer angle of his small casement; the male bringing moist clay in his beak, which the hen mixed with straws and bits of hay to form their home. As soon as the framework was completed, the pair hastened to line the interior with feathers, wool, and dried leaves; and and then flying to a neighbouring wood, they continued absent for several days.

As, however, the nest was in the course of building, two sparrows looked on with great curiosity, and no sooner had the swallows departed, than they took possession of the vacant domicile, always leaving one on the watch with his stout bill protruding through the entrance.

At length the swallows returned, when the cock made an indignant attack on the intruders, only alas! to endure a bleeding head and ruffled feathers; and so, after a short colloquy with his mate perched on a green bough, they withdrew again together. On the return of the hen sparrow, the young tutor thought that her husband gave her an account of the attack and the repulse, over which they rejoiced; and then saw them issue forth and store up a large stock of provisions, with two beaks ready to defend the entrance.

But now cries resounded in the air; crowds of swallows began to assemble on the roof; in the midst he perceived the expelled builders, recounting their wrongs to each fresh arrival; and before long two hundred of these birds were assembled. Suddenly a host of them flew against the nest—still defended by the two stout beaks—each having his bill filled with mud, which he discharged against the entrance, and then gave place to another to follow up the assault: while doing this, they so managed to accomplish, as to keep at a short distance from the nest, and be out of the reach of the besieged sparrows. The swallows now heaped mud on the nest till it was completely covered, and but for the desperate efforts of the sparrows, who contrived to shake off some of the pellets, the opening would have been soon quite choked up. But brief indeed was the interval! for a party of the swallows perched on the nest, smoothed and pressed down the clay over the opening, and soon closed it up, when loud cries arose of vengeance and victory.

Another work was yet to be done. The swallows hurried away for fresh materials; of these they constructed a nest over the blocked-up entrance, and in two hours it was occupied by the ejected swallows. No wonder the young tutor looked on with increasing interest: he observed the development of the young brood; the male bird teaching them how to seize their prey in the air—how to fly high when all was still, and the flies sported aloft—and how to keep near the ground when a storm was coming, for then all insects seek a shelter. So passed the summer, and autumn came. Crowds of swallows once more assembled on the roof of the chateau—the little birds were placed with other little birds in the midst of the troop—and ere long they all took a flight towards the east.

Spring came, and two swallows, lean and with ruffled feathers, came with it, and were recognised as the parents of the last year's brood; they repaired and re-lined the nest, and then set out on an excursion, as in the previous season. The morning after their return, a hawk pounced suddenly on the cock, and would have borne him away had not the young tutor mortally wounded the assailant with a gun. The swallow was seriously wounded by the talons of the hawk, and a grain or two of shot had grazed his breast and broken one wing. but the kind young man dressed his wounds and replaced him in the nest, while the poor hen fluttered sadly around her mate, uttering piercing cries of distress. In spite of every attention, he soon died; from that moment the hen never left her nest, refused the food that was constantly offered her, and expired five days after her beloved mate. These passages in a bird's history awakened in the mind of that young man an inextinguishable interest in Natural History; and often did he relate them when he had attained a world-wide fame as Baron Cuvier.—CASSELL'S NATURAL HISTORY.

### THE THIEVES AND THE PEASANT.

A peasant was taking a goat to Baghdad. He was mounted on a donkey, and the goat, with a bell tied round its neck, was following him. Three rogues saw this little company go past, and desired to enrich themselves.

Said the one, "May I carry off that fellow's goat in such a way that he shall never be able to ask it again of me!"

And the other cried, "Grant me the wit to rob him of the ass on which he is mounted."

"Oh, truly, what an exploit!" exclaimed the third. "What would you say if I meant so to despoil him of his clothes that he will actually be obliged to me?" The first rascal, following the traveller softly, by stealth took the bell from the goat's neck, fastened it to the ass' tail, and made off with his booty.

The man still riding the ass, heard the sound of the bell constantly behind him, and never for one instant imagined that the goat was no longer there, till bye-and-bye he happened to turn round. Picture to yourself his astonishment when he could not see the animal that he had been taking to market to sell! Of everyone who passed he asked news of his goat; presently the second rogue met him, who answered,

"At the corner of yonder lane I saw a man running off, dragging a goat along with him."

The countryman jumped from his ass, saying,

"Please take charge of my donkey," and ran after the thief in the direction he supposed him to have taken.

When he had been running hither and thither for some time, he came back to find that neither ass nor keeper were to be seen. Our two rascals had already got far away, both well content with their booty; the third leaning against a well by which the simple fellow must pass, now awaited his arrival. Then, with loud wails, he began to lament so bitterly, that the loser of the ass and goat was led to accost a person who seemed thus afflicted. Approaching him he said,—

"What are you distressed about? I am sure you cannot have had as much ill-luck as I have had; I have lost two animals, the price of which would have made my fortune."

"Oh, but think what a loss is mine!" exclaimed the thief. "Have you, like me, ever let a casket full of diamonds fall into a well when you were told to carry them to the judge? I shall, perhaps, be hanged for theft."

"But why do you not go down into the well?" asked the countryman; "it is not very deep."

"Alas! I am not clever enough," answered the rogue. "I would rather run the risk of being hanged than drown myself, which I should certainly do; but if there were any-one willing to do me this service, I would gladly give him ten pieces of gold."

"Promise me those ten pieces of gold," cried the poor dupe, thinking the sum would more than repay him for the loss of his animals, "and I will get you your casket back."

No sooner said than done; he threw off his clothes with such rapidity, and descended into the well so quickly, that the robber saw at once that he would scarcely have time to possess himself of his spoil. The countryman having reached the bottom of the well without finding any casket there,

came up again, and was speedily aware of his new misfortune. Thus, clothes, ass, and goat had all gone different ways; and their unlucky owner, with all his toil, could scarcely find people charitable enough to be willing to clothe him.—
Gozzi's Oriental Tales.

### THE PARROT AND THE KING.

Once upon a time a fowler spread a net near the nest of a parrot, and caught it therein, along with all its young ones. The parrot then said to her little ones, "My children, the best thing that can be done in this plight, is for you to lie here quite still, pretending to be dead. If this bird-catcher shall think you dead, he will leave you behind, and if I alone should be caught, then never mind. Should I remain alive, then, by one device or other, I will manage to return to you again." The young ones acted according to her advice, each continuing to lie still without drawing a breath.

The fowler, conceiving that they were probably dead, said, "Let me release them from the snare!" He accordingly threw them out of the net, whereupon, they each flew away and perched upon the branch of a tree. The bird-catcher was then enraged with the mother-parrot, and was about to dash her violently on the ground, but, just then, she exclaimed, "Oh, fowler, do not kill me! if you spare my life I will be the means of procuring you such a sum of money, that you will want for nothing all the rest of your life. As long as you shall live you will have no anxiety about anything! for I am exceedingly sagacious, and skilled in medicine. My knowledge of the medical science is as complete as anyone could desire!"

The fowler was pleased at this appeal of hers, and refrained from putting her to death. Then, addressing the bird, he said, "Parrot; the king of my country has been ill for a long time past, having a severe and obstinate disease. Do you think you could cure him?" She replied, "What is to hinder me? I am such a physician that I could restore a thousand diseased persons to health. Take me to your king and recount the praises of my healing skill—then you can sell me to him for as much as you like."

Accordingly, the fowler, having shut up the parrot in a cage, took her to his king, and said, "Your Majesty, this parrot is exceedingly sagacious, and possesses great skill in the science of medicine. If you give me the command, I will bring her into the presence of your illustrious Majesty!" The king replied, "My friend, this is just what I was anxious for: I am in great need of a wise physician, and I was just wishing that some one would come who could remove my distemper. You had better bring the bird and name her price!" He fixed it at a large sum of money, which the king ordered to be given to him. He took the money, and went home. The parrot began to administer medicine to the king, and after two or three days the king's disease was half cured thereby.

Then the parrot said, "Your Majesty, by the grace of God, and through my wisdom and medicines, you have now *half* recovered your health. If you will have compassion on me, and grant me my liberty, then, I promise you, that I will bring from the desert such an article that, in two or three days after eating it, you will be *entirely* cured." The king thought that no doubt the parrot was speaking the truth, and with this conviction, liberated her from the cage. The parrot thereupon flew off towards the forest, and joining her young ones, never showed her face again to the king.
—TALES OF A PARROT.

## CREATION.

The spacious firmament on high,
With all the blue ethereal sky,
And spangled heavens, a shining frame,
Their great Original proclaim.
The unwearied sun from day to day,
Does his Creator's power display,
And publishes to every land,
The work of an Almighty hand.
Soon as the evening shades prevail,
The moon takes up the wondrous tale,
And nightly to the listening earth,
Repeats the story of her birth:
While all the stars that round her burn,
And all the planets in their turn,
Confirm the tidings as they roll,
And spread the truth from pole to pole.
What, though in solemn silence all
Move round this dark terrestrial ball!
What, though no real voice nor sound,
Amid their radiant orbs be found!
In Reason's ear they all rejoice,
And utter forth a glorious voice;
For ever singing as they shine,
"The hand that made us is divine."—ADDISON.

## THE BOAR AND THE TWO LIONS.

One moonlight night I had taken my position on a high rock which overhung a fountain and a small marsh, a favourable spot with our hunters to watch for boars, who resorted thither to drink and root.

The moon had traversed half the heavens, and I, tired

with waiting, had fallen into a dose, when I was roused by a rustling in the wood, as on the approach of some large animal. I raised myself with caution, and examined my gun, ere the animal entered the marsh. He paused and seemed to be listening, when a half growl, half bark, announced him to be a boar; and a huge beast he was, and with stately step he entered the marsh.

I could now see by the bright moon, as he neared my station, that his bristles were white with age, and his tusks gleamed like polished steel among the dark objects around him. I got ready my gun, and waited his approach to the fountain.

Having whetted his ivory tusks, he began to root; but he appeared to be restless, as if he knew some enemy was at hand; for every now and then raising his snout, he sniffed the air.

I marvelled at these movements, for as the breeze came from a quarter opposite to my position, I knew I could not be the object of the boar's suspicion.

Now, however, I distinctly heard a slight noise near the edge of the marsh: the boar became evidently uneasy; he once or twice made a low moan, and again began to root.

Keeping a sharp look-out on the spot whence I heard the strange noise, I fancied I could distinguish the grim and shaggy head of a lion crouching upon his fore paws, and with eyes that glared like lighted charcoal through the bushes, he seemed peering at the movements of the boar. I looked again, and now I could see plainly a lion creeping cat-like on his belly as he neared the boar, who was busy rooting, but with bristles erect, and now and then muttering something that I could not understand.

The lion had crept within about twenty feet of the boar, but was hidden in part by some rushes. I waited breathless for the result; and although myself out of danger, I trembled with anxiety at the terrible scene.

The boar again raised his snout, and half turned his side towards the lion, and I fancied I could see his eye watching the enemy. Another moment, and the lion made a spring, and was received by the boar, who reared up on his hind legs. I thought I could hear the blow of his tusks as the combatants rolled on the ground. Leaning over the rock, I strained my eyes to see the result. To my surprise the boar was again on his legs, and going back a few paces, rushed at his fallen foe; a loud yell was given by the lion, which was answered by the distant howlings of the jackals. Again and again the ferocious boar charged, till he buried his very snout in the body of the lion, who was kicking in the agony of death. Blood indeed flowed from the sides of the boar, and his bristles still stood erect as he triumphed over the sultan of the forest, and now he seemed to be getting bigger and bigger. "God is great," said I, as I trembled with dread: "He will soon reach me on the rock." I threw myself flat on my face, and cried out, "There is no other God, but God, and Muhammad is his prophet!" I soon recovered my courage, and looked again. The boar had returned to his natural size, and was slaking his thirst in the fountain. I seized my gun, but reflecting, said within myself, "Why should I kill him? He will not be of any use to me; he has fought bravely, and left me the skin of a lion, and perhaps he may be a jin:* so I laid down the gun, contenting myself with thoughts of the morrow.

The boar had left the fountain, and was again busied rooting in the marsh, when another slight noise, as of a rustling in the wood, attracted my notice, and I could

* An evil genius or spirit.

perceive the smooth head of a lioness looking with surprise and horror at the body of her dead mate.

She advanced boldly. The boar stood prepared, grinding his teeth with rage. She paused, retreated to the wood, and again stopped, and lashing her tail roared with a voice that the whole wood re-echoed.

The boar stamped his hoofs, and gnashed his tusks again with rage; his bristles, red with the blood of her mate, stood on end; then lowering his snout, he rushed headlong against the lioness, who, springing aside, avoided the dread blow. A cloud came over the moon, I could not see distinctly, but I heard every blow of the paw and every rip of the tusk. There was a dead silence; again the cloud had passed, and the heavens were clear, and I saw the lioness with her fore paws on the body of the boar.

I seized my gun and aimed at her head; that was her last moment.

The morning dawned. I descended from the rock. The claw of the lioness still grasped in death the body of the boar. Many severe wounds shewed that the boar had again fought bravely.—HAY.

### THE THREE FISH.

It has been related that there was a pond at a distance from the highway, and concealed from the view of passers-by; and its hidden waters were pure like the faith of the pious, and the contemplation thereof was all-sufficient to those seeking after the fountain of life. This pool was connected with a stream of running water, and in it there abode three such beautiful fish, that *Pisces*, from envy of them, was broiled on the frying-pan of jealousy, like Aries from the heat of the sun. One of these fish was "very prudent," the second "prudent," and the other "helpless." Once upon a time, in days of spring, when the world, beautified by parterres of roses, became like the Garden of Paradise, and the earth's surface, with its bright, sweet-scented herbs, resembled the azure vault full of stars; when the chamberlain, the zephyr, had adorned the surface of the earth with carpets of various colours, and the incomparable Gardener of Creation had decked the plain of the world with roses of different hues—

The garden, from the gentle breeze, was heavy with musk,
The jessamine, in its delicacy, was like the cheek of a
  beloved one;
At the breath of the dawn the rose expands its lips,
Like a smiling beauty caressing her lover—

suddenly two or three fishermen happened to pass by that pool, and by the Divine decree discovered for a certainty the precise facts how these three fish abode in that lake. Having mutually agreed upon a rendezvous, they hastened to fetch their nets. The fish having learned this, though immersed in water, became the associates of the fire of sorrow; and when night arrived, the one who was endowed with perfect wisdom and possessed the greatest prudence— since often he had suffered violence from fortune, and the capriciousness of the tyrannical heavens, and since his foot was firmly fixed on the carpet of experience—turned in his mind the idea of escape from the net of the fishermen, and the thought of deliverance from their bonds.

> Recognise that person as wise and learned
> Who firmly establishes the basis of his proceedings;
> He whose prudence is not sound,
> The edifice of his affairs is very insecure.

He therefore quickly set about his task: and without waiting to consult his friends, went out at that place which adjoined the running stream. In the morning the fishermen, having arrived, securely blocked up both ends of the pool. The partially wise fish, who was adorned with the ornament of wisdom, but had not a share of the store of experience, when he saw what had happened, was filled with much remorse, and said, "I have been neglectful, and this is the termination of the business of the incautious. Like that other fish, I should, previous to the advent of a calamity, have been filled with anxiety on my own account, and before the attack of misfortune have devised a plan of escape.

The remedy for an occurrence should be taken before it happens;
Regret avails nought when the matter has got beyond your reach.

"Now when the season of flight is lost, it is a time for cunning and stratagem; and although it has been said that at the time of affliction deliberation no longer avails, and that in the period of misfortune no further advantage can be derived from the fruit of wisdom, yet, in spite of this, it behoveth a man of understanding not in any way to be in despair respecting the beneficial results of knowledge, nor, in repelling the devices of an enemy, to admit of any delay or procrastination." Therefore, having feigned himself to be dead, he lay drifting upon the surface of the water. A fisherman took him up, and fancying he was lifeless, threw him down on the edge of the bank. The fish, with subtlety, cast himself into the running stream and escaped safe and sound.

Die, O friend! if thou desirest freedom,
Since without dying you will not find a friend.

The other fish, in whose affairs negligence was predominant, and in whose actions incapacity was apparent, bewildered and stupefied, confounded and irresolute, went from right to left, and darted up and down, till at last he was captured.—FABLES OF BIDPAI.

### MURAD THE UNLUCKY.

It was hot weather and my thirst was excessive. I went out with a party, in hopes of finding a spring of water. The English soldiers began to dig for a well, in a place pointed out to them by one of their men of science. I was not inclined to such hard labour, but preferred sauntering on in search of a spring. I saw at a distance something that looked like a pool of water; and I pointed it out to my companions. Their man of science warned me by his interpreter, not to trust to this deceitful appearance; for that such were common in this country, and that, when I came close to the spot, I should find no water there. He added, that it was at a greater distance than I imagined, and that I should in all probability be lost in the desert if I attempted to follow this phantom. I was so unfortunate as not to attend to his advice. I set out in pursuit of this accursed delusion, which assuredly was the work of evil spirits, who clouded my reason, and allured me into their dominion. I went on, hour after hour, in expectation continually of reaching the object of my wishes; but it fled faster than I pursued, and I discovered at last that the Englishman, who had doubtless gained his information from the people of the country, was right; and that the shining appearance, which I had taken for water, was a mere deception.

I was now exhausted with fatigue: I looked back in vain after the companions I had left; I could see neither men, animals, nor any trace of vegetation in the sandy desert. I had no resource but, weary as I was, to measure back my footsteps, which were imprinted in the sand.

I sorrowfully and slowly traced them as my guides in this unknown land. Instead of yielding to my indolent inclinations, I ought, however, to have made the best of my way back, before the evening breeze sprung up. I felt the breeze rising, and unconscious of my danger, I rejoiced, and opened my bosom to meet it; but what was my dismay when I saw that the wind swept before it all trace of my footsteps in the sand. I knew not which way to proceed; I was struck with despair, tore my garments, threw off my turban and cried aloud; but neither human voice nor echo answered me. The silence was dreadful. I had tasted no food for many hours, and I now became sick and faint. I recollected that I had put a supply of opium into the folds of my turban; but, alas! when I took my turban up I found that the opium had fallen out. I searched for it in vain on the sand, where I had thrown the turban. I stretched myself out upon the ground, and yielded without further struggle to my evil destiny. What I suffered from thirst, hunger, and heat, cannot be described. At last I fell into a sort of trance, during which images of various kinds seemed to flit before my eyes. How long I remained in this state I know not: but I remember that I was brought to my senses by a loud shout, which came from persons belonging to a caravan returning from Mecca. This was a shout of joy for their safe arrival at a certain spring, well known to them in this part of the desert. The spring was not a hundred yards from the spot where I lay; yet such had been the fate of Murad the unlucky, that he missed the reality, whilst he had been hours in pursuit of the phantom. Feeble and spiritless as I was, I sent forth as loud a cry as I could, in hopes of obtaining assistance; and I endeavoured to crawl to the place from which the voices appeared to come. The caravan rested for a considerable time, whilst the slaves filled the skins with water, and whilst the camels took in their supply. I worked myself on towards them; yet, notwithstanding my efforts, I was persuaded that according to my usual ill fortune I should never be able to make them hear my voice. I saw them mount their camels! I took off my turban, unrolled it, and waved it in the air. My signal was seen, The caravan came towards me.—EDGEWORTH.

## THE CHOICE OF HERCULES.

When Hercules was in that part of his youth, in which it was natural for him to consider what course of life he ought to pursue, he one day retired into a desert, where the silence and solitude of the place very much favoured his meditations. As he was musing on his present condition, and very much perplexed in himself on the course of life he should choose, he saw two women of a larger stature than ordinary, approaching toward him. One of them had a very noble air, and graceful deportment: her beauty was natural and easy, her person clear and unspotted, her eyes cast toward the ground with an agreeable reserve, her motion and behaviour full of modesty, and her raiment as white as snow. The other had a great deal of health and floridness in her countenance, which she had helped with an artificial white and red; and endeavoured to appear more graceful than ordinary in her mien, by a mixture of affectation in all her gestures. She had a wonderful confidence and assurance in her looks, and all the variety o colours in her dress that she thought were the most proper to show her complexion to advantage. She cast her eyes upon herself, then turned them on those that were present, to see how they liked her, and often looked on the figure she made in her shadow. Upon her nearer approach to Hercules, she stepped before the other lady, who came forward with a regular composed carriage, and running up to him, accosted him after the following manner;—

"My dear Hercules," said she, "I find you are very much divided in your own thoughts upon the way of life that you ought to choose: be my friend, and follow me; I will lead you into the possession of pleasure, and out of the reach of pain, and remove you from all the noise and disquietude of business. The affairs of either war or peace shall have no power to disturb you. Your whole employment shall be to make your life easy, and to entertain every sense with its proper gratifications. Sumptuous tables, beds of roses, clouds of perfumes, concerts of music, crowds of beauties, are all in readiness to receive you. Come along with me into this region of delights, this world of pleasure, and bid farewell for ever to care, to pain, to business."

Hercules hearing the lady talk after this manner, desired to know her name; to which she answered, "My friends, and those who are well acquainted with me, call me Happiness: but my enemies, and those who would injure my reputation, have given me the name of Pleasure."

By this time the other lady had come up, and addressed herself to the young hero in a very different manner.

"Hercules," said she, "I offer myself to you, because I know you are descended from the gods, and give proofs of that descent by your love of virtue, and application to the studies proper for your age. This makes me hope you will gain, both for yourself and me, an immortal reputation. But, before I invite you into my society and friendship, I will be open and sincere with you, and must lay down this as an established truth, that there is nothing truly valuable which can be purchased without pains and labour. The gods have set a price upon every real and noble pleasure. If you would gain the favour of the Deity, you must be at the pains of worshipping him; if the friendship of good men, you must study to oblige them—if you would be honoured by your country, you must take care to serve it. In short, if you would be eminent in war or peace, you must become master of all the qualifications that can make you so. These are the only terms and conditions upon which I can propose happiness." The Goddess of Pleasure here broke in upon her discourse: "You see," said she, "Hercules, by her own confession, the way to her pleasures is long and difficult, whereas that which I propose is short and easy." "Alas!" said the other lady, whose visage glowed with passion made up of scorn and pity, "what are the pleasures you propose? To eat before you are hungry, drink before you are athirst, sleep before you are tired: to gratify appetites before they are raised, and raise such appetites as nature never planted. You never heard the most delicious music, which is the praise of one's self; or saw the most beautiful object, which is the work of one's own hands. Your votaries pass away their youth in a dream of mistaken pleasures, while they are hoarding up anguish, torment, and remorse for old age.

"As for me, I am the friend of the gods and of good men, an agreeable companion to the artizan, a household guardian to the fathers of families, a patron and protector of servants, an associate of all true and generous friendships. The banquets of my votaries are never coslty, but always delicious; for none eat or drink at them who are not invited by hunger and thirst. Their slumbers are sound, and their wakings cheerful. My young men have the pleasure of hearing themselves praised by those who are in years,—and those who are in years, of being honoured by those who are young. In a word, my followers are favoured by the gods, beloved by their acquaintance, esteemed by their country, and, after the close of their labours, honoured by posterity."

We know, by the life of this memorable hero, to which of these two ladies he gave up his heart; and, I believe, every one who reads this will do him the justice to approve his choice.—ADDISON.

### THE VANITY OF RICHES.

As Ortogrul of Basra was one day wandering along the streets of Baghdad, musing on the varieties of merchandise which the shops offered to his view, and observing the different occupations which busied the multitudes on every side, he was awakened from the tranquillity of meditation by a crowd that obstructed his passage. He raised his eyes, and saw the chief vizier, who having returned from the divan, was entering his palace.

Ortogrul mingled with the attendants, and being supposed to have some petition for the vizier, was permitted to enter. He surveyed the spaciousness of the apartments, admired the walls hung with golden tapestry, and the floors covered with silken carpets, and despised the single neatness of his own little habitation.

Surely said he to himself, this palace is the seat of happiness, where pleasure succeeds to pleasure, and discontent and sorrow can have no admission. Whatever nature has provided for the delight of sense, is here spread forth to be enjoyed. What can mortals hope or imagine, which the master of this palace has not obtained? The dishes of luxury cover his table, the voice of harmony lulls him in his bowers: he breathes the fragrance of the groves of Java, and sleeps upon the down of the swans of the Ganges. He speaks, and his mandate is obeyed; he wishes, and his wish is gratified: all whom he sees obey him, and all whom he sees flatter him. How different, Ortogrul, is thy condition, who art doomed to the perpetual torments of unsatisfied desire, and who hath no amusement in thy power that can withhold thee from thy own reflections! They tell thee that thou art wise: but what does wisdom avail with poverty? None will flatter the poor, and the wise have very little power of flattering themselves. That man is surely the most wretched of the sons of wretchedness, who lives with his own faults and follies always before him, who has none to reconcile him to himself by praise and veneration. I have long sought content, and have not found it; I will from this moment endeavour to be rich.

Full of his new resolution, he shut himself in his chamber for six months, to deliberate how he should grow rich; he sometimes proposed to offer himself as a counsellor to one of the kings of India, and sometimes resolved to dig for diamonds in the mines of Golconda. One day, after some hours passed in violent fluctuation of opinion, sleep insensibly seized him in his chair; he dreamed that he was ranging a desert country in search of some one that might teach him to grow rich; and as he stood on the top of a hill shaded with cypress, in doubt whither to direct his steps, his father appeared on a sudden standing before him. "Ortogrul," said the old man, "I know thy perplexity; listen to thy father; turn thine eye on the opposite mountain." Ortogrul looked, and saw a torrent tumbling down the rocks, roaring with a voice of thunder, and scattering its foam on the impending woods. "Now," said his father, "behold the valley that lies between the hills." Ortogrul looked, and espied a little well out of which issued a small rivulet. "Tell me, now," said his father, "dost thou wish for sudden affluence, that may pour upon thee like the mountain torrent, or for a slow and gradual increase, resembling the rill gliding from the well?" "Let me be quickly rich," said Ortogrul, "let the golden stream be quick and violent." "Look around thee," said his father, "once again." Ortogrul looked and perceived the channel of the torrent dry and dusty; but following the rivulet from the well, he traced it to a wide lake, which the supply, slow and constant, kept always full. He waked, and determined to grow rich by silent profit, and persevering industry.

Having sold his patrimony, he engaged in merchandise, and in twenty years purchased lands, on which he raised a house, equal in sumptuousness to that of the vizier, to which he invited all the ministers of pleasure, expecting to enjoy all the felicity which he had imagined riches able to afford. Leisure soon made him weary of himself, and he longed to be persuaded that he was great and happy. He was courteous and liberal; he gave all that approached him hopes of pleasing him, and all who should please him hopes of being rewarded. Every art of praise was tried, and every source of adulatory fiction was exhausted. Ortogrul heard his flatterers without delight, because he found himself unable to believe them. His own heart told him its frailties, his own understanding reproached him with his faults. "How long," said he with a deep sigh, "have I been labouring in vain to amass wealth which at last is useless? Let no man hereafter wish to be rich, who is already too wise to be flattered."—JOHNSON.

## THE SPIDER.

I perceived, about four years ago, a large spider in one corner of my room, making its web; and though the maid frequently levelled her fatal broom against the labours of the little animal, I had the good fortune to prevent its destruction, and I may say, it more than paid me by the entertainment it afforded.

In three days the web was with incredible diligence completed; nor could I avoid thinking that the insect seemed to exult in its new abode. It frequently traversed it round, examined the strength of every part of it, retired into its hole, and came out very frequently. The first enemy, however, it had to encounter, was another and a much larger spider, which, having no web of its own, and having probably exhausted all its stock in former labours of this kind, came to invade the property of its neighbour. Soon then a terrible encounter ensued, in which the invader seemed to have the victory, and the laborious spider was obliged to take refuge in its hole. Upon this I perceived the victor using every art to draw the enemy from his stronghold. He seemed to go off, but quickly returned, and when he found all arts vain, began to demolish the new web without mercy. This brought on another battle, and contrary to my expectations, the laborious spider became conqueror, and fairly killed his antagonist.

Now then, in peaceable possession of what was justly its own, it waited three days with the utmost impatience, repairing the breaches of its web, and taking no sustenance that I could perceive. At last, however, a large blue fly fell into the snare, and struggled hard to get loose. The spider gave it leave to entangle itself as much as possible, but it seemed to be too strong for the cobweb. I must own I was greatly surprised when I saw the spider immediately sally out, and in less than a minute weave a new net round its captive, by which the motion of its wings was stopped, and when it was fairly hampered in this manner, it was seized, and dragged into the hole.

In this manner it lived in a precarious state, and nature seemed to have fitted it for such a life: for upon a single fly it subsisted for more than a week. I once put a wasp into the nest, but when the spider came out in order to seize it as usual, upon perceiving what kind of an enemy it had to deal with, it instantly broke all the bands that held it fast, and contributed all that lay in its power to disengage so formidable an antagonist. When the wasp was at liberty, I expected the spider would have set about repairing the breaches that were made in its net, but those it seems were irreparable, wherefore the cobweb was now entirely forsaken, and a new one begun, which was completed in the usual time.

I had now a mind to try how many cobwebs a single spider could furnish; wherefore I destroyed this, and the insect set about another. When I destroyed the other also, its whole stock seemed entirely exhausted, and it could spin no more. The arts it made use of to support itself, now deprived of its great means of subsistence, were indeed surprising. I have seen it roll up its legs like a ball, and lie motionless for hours together, but cautiously watching all the time; when a fly happened to approach sufficiently near, it would dart out all at once, and often seize its prey.

Of this life, however, it soon began to grow weary, and resolved to invade the possession of some other spider, since it could not make a web of its own. It formed an attack upon a neighbouring fortification with great vigour, and at first was as vigorously repulsed. Not daunted, however, with one defeat, in this manner it continued to lay siege to another's web for three days, and at length, having killed the defendant, actually took possession. When smaller flies happen to fall into the snare, the spider does not sally out at once, but very patiently waits till it is sure of them; for upon his immediately approaching, the terror of his appearance might give the captive strength sufficient to get loose: the manner then is to wait patiently till, by ineffectual and impotent struggles, the captive has wasted all its strength, and then it becomes a certain and easy conquest.

The insect I am now describing lived three years; every year it changed its skin, and got a new set of legs. I have sometimes plucked off a leg, which grew again in two or three days. At first it dreaded my approach to its web, but at last it became so familiar as to take a fly out of my hand, and upon my touching any part of the web, would immediately leave its hole, prepared either for a defence or an attack.—GOLDSMITH.

### SCENES IN INDIA.

I stood under the shade of a large banian tree, enjoying the sight; when suddenly I felt from behind a blow on my head, which stunned me. I fell to the ground; and, when I came to my senses, found myself in the hands of four armed soldiers, and a black, who was pulling my diamond ring from my finger. They were carrying me away amid the cries and lamentations of the slaves, who followed us. "Stand off! it is in vain you shriek," said one of the soldiers to the surrounding crowd: "What we do is by order of the Sultan. Thus he punishes traitors."

Without further explanation, I was thrown into a dungeon belonging to the governor of the mines, who stood by with insulting joy to see me chained to a large stone in my horrid prison. I knew him to be my enemy: but what was my astonishment when I recollected in the countenance of the black, who was fastening my chains and loading me with curses, that very Saheb, whose life I had formerly saved. To all my questions no answer was given, but "It is the will of the Sultan;" or, "Thus the Sultan avenges himself on traitors."

The door of my dungeon was then locked and barred, and I was left alone in perfect darkness. Is this, thought I, the reward of all my faithful services? Bitterly did I regret that I was not in my native country, where no man at the will of a Sultan can be thrown into a dungeon without knowing his crime, or his accusers. I cannot attempt to describe to you what I felt during this most miserable day of my existence. Feeble at last for want of food, I stretched myself out, as well as my chains would allow me, and tried to compose myself to sleep. I sunk into a state of insensibility, in which I must have remained for several hours, for it was midnight when I was roused by the unbarring of my prison door. It was the black, Saheb, who entered, carrying in one hand a torch, and in the other some food, which he set before me in silence. I cast upon him a look of scorn, and was about to reproach him with his ingratitude, when he threw himself at my feet, and burst into tears. "Is it possible," said he to me, "that you are not sure of the heart of Saheb! You saved my life; I am come to save yours. But eat, master," continued he, "eat whilst I speak, for we have no time to lose. To-morrow's sun must see us far from hence. You cannot support the fatigues you have to undergo without taking food." I yielded to his entreaties, and, whilst I ate, Saheb informed me that my imprisonment was owing to the treacherous Hindoo merchant, Omychund; who, in hopes I suppose of possessing himself in quiet of all the wealth which I had entrusted to his care, went to the Sultan and accused me of having secreted certain diamonds of great value, which he pretended I had shown to him in confidence. Tippoo, enraged at this, dispatched immediate orders to four of his soldiers, to go in search of me, seize me, imprison and torture me, till I should confess where these diamonds were concealed. Saheb was in the Sultan's apartment when this order was given, and immediately hastened to Prince Abdulcalie, whom he knew to be my friend, and informed him of what had happened. The Prince sent for Omychund, and, after carefully questioning, was convinced by his contradictory answers and by his confusion, that the charge against me was wholly unfounded. He dismissed Omychund, however, without letting him know his opinion, and then sent Saheb for the four soldiers, who were setting out in search of me. In their presence he gave Saheb orders aloud to take charge of me, the moment I should be found, and secretly commissioned him to favour my escape. The soldiers thought that in obeying the Prince they obeyed the Sultan; and consequently, when I was taken and lodged in my dungeon, the keys of it were delivered to Saheb. When he had finished telling me all this, he restored to me my ring, which he said he snatched from my finger as soon as I was seized, that I might not be robbed of it by the governor, or some of the soldiers.

The grateful Saheb now struck off my chains; and my own anxiety for my escape was scarcely equal to his. He had swift horses belonging to the soldiers in readiness: and we pursued our course all night without interruption. He was well acquainted with the country, having accompanied the Sultan on several expeditions. When we thought ourselves beyond the reach of all pursuers, Saheb permitted me to rest; but I never rested at my ease till I was out of Tippoo Sultàn's dominions, and once more in safety at Madras.—EDGEWORTH.

### ADVICE TO YOUNG MEN.

The most usual way among young men who have no resolution of their own, is first to ask one friend's advice, and follow it for some time; then, to ask advice of another, and turn to that; so of a third; still unsteady, always changing. However, every change of this nature is for the worse: people may tell you of your being unfit for some peculiar occupations in life; but heed them not. Whatever employment you follow with perseverance and assiduity, will be found fit for you; it will be your support in youth and comfort in age. . . . . In learning the useful part of every trade, very moderate abilities will suffice: great abilities are generally an obstacle to success. . . . . Be contented with one good employment: for, if you understand two at a time, people will give you business in neither.

A conjuror and a tailor once happening to converse together, "Alas!" cries the tailor, "what an unhappy poor creature am I! If people take it into their heads to live without clothes, I am undone; I have no other trade to have recourse to." "Indeed, friend! I pity you sincerely," replies the conjuror; "but, thank Heaven! things are not quite so bad with me: for, if one trick should fail, I have a hundred tricks more for them yet. However, if at any time you are reduced to beggary, apply to me, and I will relieve you." A famine overspread the land; the tailor made a shift to live, because his customers could not be without clothes! but the poor conjuror, with all his hundred tricks, could find none that had any money to throw away. It was in vain that he promised to eat fire, or to vomit pins; no single creature would relieve him, till he was at last obliged to beg from the very tailor whose calling he had formerly despised.

There are no obstructions more fatal to success than pride and resentment. The resentment of a poor man is like the efforts of a harmless insect to sting; it may get him crushed, but cannot defend him. Who values that anger which is consumed only in empty menaces?

Once upon a time a goose fed its young by a pond side; and a goose, in such circumstances, is always extremely proud, and excessively punctilious. If any other animal, without the least design to offend, happened to pass that way, the goose was immediately at it. "The pond," she said, "was hers, and she would maintain her right in it, and support her honour, while she had a bill to hiss, or a wing to flutter. In this manner she drove away ducks, pigs, and chickens; nay, even the insidious cat was seen to scamper away from her. A mastiff, however, happened to pass by, and thought it no harm if he should drink a little of the water, as he was thirsty. The goose flew at him, pecked at him with her beak, and slapped him with her feathers. The dog grew angry, and had twenty times a mind to give her a sly snap; but suppressing his indignation, because his master was nigh, "Shame on thee!" cries he, "for a fool! sure those who have neither strength nor weapons to fight, at least should be civil." So saying, he went forward to the pond, quenched his thirst in spite of the goose, and followed his master.

Another obstruction to the fortune of youth is, that, while they are willing to take offence from none, they are also equally desirous of giving nobody offence. Hence, they endeavour to please all, comply with every request, and attempt to suit themselves to every company; have no will of their own, but like wax, readily catch every impression. By thus attempting to give universal satisfaction, they at last find themselves miserably disappointed: to bring the generality of admirers on one's side, it is enough to produce good workmanship. A painter of eminence once had resolved to finish a piece which should please the whole world. When, therefore, he had drawn a picture, in which his utmost skill was exhausted, it was exposed in the public market-place, with directions at the bottom for every spectator to mark with a brush that lay by, every limb and feature which seemed erroneous. The spectators came, and in general applauded; but each, willing to show his talent at criticism, marked whatever he thought proper. At evening, when the painter came, he was mortified to find the picture one universal blot—not a single stroke that had not the marks of disapprobation. Not satisfied with this trial, the next day he was resolved to try them in a different manner: and, exposing his picture as before, desired that every spectator would mark those beauties he approved or admired. The people complied, and the artist returning, found his picture covered with the marks of beauty; every stroke that had been yesterday condemned, now received the character of approbation. "Well," cries the painter, "I now find that the best way to succeed is to aim at satisfying the few."—GOLDSMITH.

### THE CHAMOIS, AND CHAMOIS HUNTING.

The animals which lend the greatest charm to the mountains are the chamois; those beautiful, swift-footed goats of the rock, which wander in small herds through the loneliest districts of the Alps, people the highest ridges, and course rapidly over leagues of ice-fields. Though much resembling the goat, the chamois is distinguished from it by longer and larger legs, a longer neck, a shorter and more compact body, and especially by its horns, which are black and curved like a hook. These horns are much used in ornamenting those ingenious fabrics which the Swiss peasants make, and which travellers bring back as memorials from that country.

They live together in herds of five, ten, or twenty. Their grace and agility are very remarkable. They bound across wide and deep chasms, and balance themselves on the most difficult ledges; then, throwing themselves on their hind legs, reach securely the landing place, often no bigger than a man's hand, on which their unerring eye has been fixed. It is difficult to give a trustworthy account of this noble animal's agility.

Their wonderful sense of smell, sight, and hearing, preserves the chamois from many perils. When they are collected in troops, they will appoint a doe as sentinel, which grazes alone at a little distance, while the others are feeding; and looks round every instant snuffing the air with her nose. If she perceives any danger, she gives a shrill whistle, and the rest fly after her at a gallop. But their most acute sense is that of smell. They scent the hunter from an immense distance if he stands in the direction of the wind. The trained chamois hunters of Switzerland belong to the poorer classes. They are a sturdy frugal race, inured to all weathers, and familiar with the details of the mountains, the habits of the animals, and the art of hunting them. The hunter needs a sharp eye, a steady hand, a robust frame, a spirit resolute, calm, ready and circumspect; and besides all this, good lungs and untiring energy. He must be not only a first-rate shot, but also a first-rate climber; for the chamois hunter often finds himself in positions where he must exert every limb and muscle to the utmost, in order to support or push himself forward.

The ordinary preparations of the hunter consist of a warm dress, with a cap, a strong Alpine staff, a pouch with powder, bullets, and telescope, bread and cheese, and a little flask of spirits. In order to procure something warm, he takes an iron bowl and a portion of meal, baked beforehand, and mixes it with water over a fire. But the most essential parts of the equipment are a pair of stout mountain shoes and a gun.

The hunter starts by starlight in the evening, or at midnight, in order to gain the highest hunting ground before sunrise. He knows the haunts of the animals, their favourite pastures and hiding-places, and directs his course accordingly. The principal point is always to keep the animals before the wind; for should the lightest breeze be wafted before him to the chamois, the creature scents him at an immense distance, and is lost. Many hours of patient waiting and watching must be passed before he can get within shot of them.

The chase is not only toilsome, but dangerous. The hunter is often led by the eagerness of his pursuit to the brink of fearful precipices, where a single false step may cause instant death; or to narrow ridges of rock and slippery ice, where it is hard to find firm footing, and where a fall might be fatal. Sometimes he is allured to a spot where he can neither advance nor recede. Sometimes a sharp frost overtakes the weary hunter, and cramps his limbs. If he yields to an almost unconquerable impulse to sit down, he immediately falls asleep, never to wake again.

Sometimes a large falling stone wounds him or dashes him into the abyss; or an avalanche overwhelms him, and buries him deep beneath the snow. But no enemy is more dangerous than the fog, when it surprises him in the awful labyrinth of peaks, leagues and leagues above the dwellings of man, closing in so thickly that often he cannot see six feet before him, and must inevitably be lost unless great presence of mind and local knowledge can extricate him from the peril. His situation is yet worse if the fog be followed by a snow-storm covering up every track on the ground before him.

The actual profits of the chase bear no proportion to the perils, labour, and loss of time which it involves. And yet the hunters have a perfect passion for the sport. One at Zurich, who had his leg cut off, gratefully sent his surgeon, two years afterwards, half of a chamois which he had killed, remarking at the same time that the chase did not get on so well with a wooden leg, but he hoped to kill many a chamois yet. This man was seventy-one years old when he lost his leg. A guide once said to a traveller on the Alps; "A short time since I made a very happy marriage. My father and grandfather both met their end in chamois-hunting, and I feel convinced I shall perish in the same manner, but if you would make my fortune, on condition I should never hunt, I could not accept it." Two years afterwards he fell down a precipice, and was dashed in pieces.

It has been often remarked that this occupation exercises a decided influence on the character of the hunter. Undoubtedly the constant warfare with peril, hunger, thirst, and cold, which it entails, and the patience, resolution, and dexterity which it calls into such constant practice, must after ten or twenty years of life, mark the tone of thought and feeling in no slight degree. Accordingly we find the chamois hunter generally silent, prompt, and decided in word and action, and at the same time temperate, frugal, contented, and easily reconciled to unavoidable evils.—ANON.

### VALOUR.

The young Baron de Villetreton, in entering amongst the gentlemen who formed the household guard of the king of France in 1745, not only gained by his exemplary conduct, the esteem of his officers, and the friendship of his comrades, but attracted the attention of the monarch himself. One alone among his comrades, M. de Malatour, took umbrage at this high and general favour, and on the occasion of some trifling expression or gesture, publicly insulted him. Villetreton refused to challenge him, as being contrary to his principles, but determined that this seeming cowardice in not fighting a well-known swordsman, should be redeemed by some distinguished act during the campaign just commenced. That moment soon arrived; and for his brave conduct in taking the colours at the battle of Fonteny, he was honoured with the cross of St. Louis from the king's own hand on the field, and received the eulogium of Marshal Saxe, but encountered in consequence, a redoubled enmity on the part of M. de Malatour.

On arriving at his estate, the baron called his old hunter, ascertained that in the district of one of the lofty peaks covered with snow, there were five bears, and arranged for a chase in about a week.

"Do you know," he said "hunter, some of my comrades are rather good sportsmen; there is one of them who is able to hit a candle at eighty yards?"

"Easier, perhaps, than to kill a bear at ten," replied the old man laughing.

"That is what I said also. But as I should wish to judge for myself of his powers, you must place us together at the same post—at the bridge of Maure, for instance."

"Ah!" said the hunter, scratching his ear, "it would better please me to have you elsewhere."

"Why?"

"Because, to guard this post, a man will be between two deaths—the bears and the precipice."

"I know the one and do not fear the other," said the baron.

A few days afterwards, all those invited, not excepting De Malatour, who, notwithstanding the delicate attentions of his host, maintained a cold reserve, assembled at the château. The next morning, as the large hunting party reached the crest of the mountain which immediately overhung it, the first rays of the sun breaking from the east glanced on the summit of the Pyrenees, and suddenly illuminating the landscape, displayed beneath them a deep valley, covered with majestic pine-trees, which murmured in the fresh breeze of the morning.

Opposite to them, the foaming waters of a cascade fell for some hundreds of feet through a cleft which divided the mountain from the summit to the base. By some remote convulsion the chasm was surmounted by a natural bridge—the piles of granite at each side being joined by one immense flat rock. Sinister legends were associated with the place, and the mountaineers recounted with terror, that no hunter, with the exception of the baron's, had ever been posted at the bridge of Maure, without becoming the prey of the bears or the precipice. The hunter, on the other hand, attributed the fatality to its real cause—the dizziness arising from the sight of the precipice and the bears, so that the hunter's presence of mind was destroyed, his aim became unsteady, and his death the inevitable consequence. He could not, however, altogether divest himself of fears for his young master, who obstinately persevered in his intention to occupy the bridge, with De Malatour.

After placing the baron's companions at posts which he considered the most advantageous, the hunter rejoined his men, and disposing them so as to encompass the valley facing the cascade, commanded the utmost silence to be observed until they should hear the first bark of his dog. The silence remained unbroken for some minutes, when suddenly a furious barking commenced, the dogs were let loose, trumpets, drums, saucepans, and other discordant instruments were in full play, every gun was ready, and all moved slowly forwards, contracting the circle as they approached the cascade, while the growling of the bears mingled with the clamour, which, rolling along the sides of the valley was repeated by distant echoes. At this moment, the young baron, standing on the bridge, looked at his companion, whose countenance, though pale, remained calm and scornful.

"Attention, sir!" said he in a low voice. "The bears are not far from us: let your aim be true, or else——"

"Keep your counsels for yourself, sir!"

"Attention," repeated Villetreton, without seeming to notice the surly response, "he approaches."

Those who were placed in the front of the cascade, seeing the bears directing their course to the bridge, cried out from all parts, "Look out, look out, Villetreton!" But the breaking of branches, followed by the rolling of loosened stones down the precipice, had already given warning of the animal's near approach. Malatour now became deadly pale, but grasped his gun as if he were a resolute hunter.

A bear now appeared, with foaming mouth and glaring eyes, at times turning as if he would gladly struggle with his pursuers; but when he saw his only way of escape—the bridge—occupied, he growled terribly, and raised himself on his hind legs, was rushing on Villetreton and Malatour, when a ball struck him in the forehead, and he fell dead at their feet.

Malatour convulsively grasped his gun; he had become completely powerless; when suddenly new cries, louder and more pressing, were heard, "Fire! fire! he is on you!" shouted the hunter, who appeared unexpectedly, pale and agitated, his gun to his shoulder, but afraid to fire, lest he should wound or kill his master.

Villetreton, perceiving his agitation, turned round. It was indeed time. On the other side of the bridge, a bear, much larger than than the first, was in the act of making a final rush. Springing forward, the baron seized the gun of his terrified companion, and instantly lodged its contents in the breast of the bear, which rolled, in the death struggle, to where they stood. All this was the work of a moment. Even the knees of the hardy old hunter shook with emotion at his master's escape; as for Malatour, his livid paleness and convulsive shudderings told their own tale.

"Take your weapon," said the baron, quickly giving him the carbine: "here are our comrades, they must not see you unarmed; and, hunter, not a word of all this." "Look!" said he to his companions as they gathered around, pointing to the monstrous beasts, "one to each. Now, M. de Malatour, I wait your orders." The latter made no reply, but stretched out his hand, which Villetreton cordially shook.

That evening a banquet was given to celebrate the

double victory. Towards the close of the evening Malatour rose up and exclaimed, " It was M. Villetreton alone who killed the two bears ; and if, through his generosity, I have allowed the illusion to last so long, it was simply because the affront which I gave him was a public one, and the reparation ought to be public likewise. I now declare that M. de Villetreton is the bravest of the brave, and that I shall maintain it towards all and against all."—CASSELL's NATURAL HISTORY.

### A BOAR HUNT.

On arriving at the field, a little before sunset, we found the owners with a pack of curs preparing to scare away the boar; and they told us it was no use firing at him, for there was not a huntsman of any fame in the neighbourhood who had not had a shot, but without success. It was, they said, as much as they could do to prevent the beast destroying all the melons, as he cared little for either dogs or men; nay, he would stay quietly at the border of the wood, until he found an occasion for rushing in to seize a melon, with which he would make off into the thicket; and, when dogs and men were tired with watching and overcome by sleep, he would boldly enter the ground and bite, as if for mere spite, a piece out of every melon that was fit to eat. In fact, they thought him to be some evil-disposed jin (spirit), and therefore it might be even an unholy act to kill him; for there was no knowing, some whispered, what might happen in such a case.

"Well," said I, "let me try my hand, and if I fail, as others have done, I will pay for every melon he destroys: but I hope for success."

"Allah Akbar" (God is great), said one of the melon-growers: "if, Christian, you only saw his tusks, and how he puts up his bristles when he enters the field, you would wish yourself in Tangier again!" "But come," said they, "make ready for the sun is nearly set, and you may be certain the boar is now listening to all we are saying."

I was now conducted to a pomegranate bush, near which there were some ripe melons. Here I was to station myself; and, by sitting cross-legged on the ground, I was partly hidden by some long grass. Ali Safar wished to be my companion, but I preferred, as I always do at night-hunts, to be alone, being thus more likely to keep awake.

"May God preserve you!" said the party, as they took their leave; "and take care," they added, "not to sleep. We shall be within hearing of your shot, and will come to your assistance the moment you fire."

"Well, good night!" I replied, and I arranged myself for the attack.

The sound of the Moor's footsteps had scarcely died away, when a slight crackling in the wood drew my attention; and soon I heard, and plainly, the rooting and the footsteps of some large animal.

"At any rate," thought I, "he does not move like a supernatural being." Whilst I was waiting in this state of excitement for the boar's approach, I heard the tread of a man's foot in a different direction from that by which the party had retired; and shortly I saw a long gun-barrel glisten in the twilight, over the hedge. When the man who carried it reached the low gate, and had cautiously thrown it open, he looked into the field, and then, to my surprise, and some fear too, he levelled his long gun exactly at the spot where I was sitting. In a moment I pointed my gun at his head, and called out in Arabic, "Who is there?"

"Your better," was the reply.

"That," I retorted, "remains to be proved. Down with your gun, or I fire!"

"Son of the English," said the hunter, who recognised my voice, "thank God! I did not fire; but you looked so very like a boar, as you sat under the pomegranate bush, that I was just going to shoot when you called out."

"I fear," said I to the hunter, who proved to be no other than my friend Hajji Abdallah, "you have spoiled my sport, for the boar will have made off."

"No, no," he said, "I have fired at this boar half-a-dozen times in the same night; he is now listening to what we are saying; and when we have ceased to make a noise, he will come in for his melon just as if nobody was here, and carry it off to the wood."

I now begged him to join the rest of the party, for I wished to be alone, and accordingly he took his leave.

The last rays of daylight had now disappeared—the night was cold—there was no moon—and the stars, usually bright in this climate, were dimmed by clouds: the wood began to echo with the howlings of jackals, searching for their prey—and soon the dull sound of the evening-gun at Gibraltar reached my ears, and told it was nine o'clock. I had given up all hope of the boar returning, when a dark shadow passed rapidly across the field, and, retreating to the wood, rather startled me. I then heard the munching of a melon. "That was cleverly done," thought I, "and jin-like; but try such a manœuvre again, my fine fellow, and I will be your match."

Some minutes elapsed and again the same dark shadow passed, stopped for a moment, and then made towards the wood. I determined, however, not to fire till I could get a near shot; and I thought that, perhaps, the animal hearing no noise, would be less rapid in his movements. Again and again the same thing occurred: and I was counting the number of melons he would manage to destroy before the morning, and for which I should have to pay, when the boar, entering as before, stopped, and began to blow, and make the low moan which the Moors interpret, "I hope there is no treachery." I aimed my gun at his head, which was towards me; but he was too far off for me to fire at him on a dark night. Taking courage on finding no dog to molest him, he began to root quite at his ease, and gradually neared the spot where I was posted, till he came within paces.

I held my breath, and got ready my gun; his whole side was turned towards me: I aimed at his shoulder, I then lowered my gun to be sure that my aim was good; again I pointed, again I lowered it; a third time I levelled, fired, and threw myself flat on my face. I heard the beast rush by me, and, as it appeared to me, fall some twenty yards beyond: there was a slight kicking for a few moments, and then all was quiet. Still lying on the ground, I quietly loaded my gun, and half raised myself, to see if I could make him out.

The owners of the field and Ali Safar soon joined me. I told them what I had done, but they would not believe that the animal was wounded.

"Take care!" said I, "of yourselves; for he may be on the top of us before we are aware."

"Where," said one of them, "did you hear him last?"

I led the man to the spot amid some long grass.

"There ought to be blood hereabouts, then, if the animal is wounded," said he, putting down his hand. As he did this he started back, and ran off, shouting "E'Shaitan, E'Shaitan" (the Devil, the Devil). I put my gun down, and found that there was the boar, but the beast was quite dead.

They would hardly credit my success at first, but when they discovered the monster to be truly dead, they were most eloquent in their praises.—HAY.

## THE BURIAL OF SIR JOHN MOORE.

Not a drum was heard, not a funeral note
   As his corpse to the ramparts we hurried;
Not a soldier discharged his farewell shot
   O'er the grave where our hero we buried.

We buried him darkly at dead of night,
   The sods with our bayonets turning,
By the struggling moonbeams' misty light,
   And the lantern dimly burning.

No useless coffin enclosed his breast,
   Nor in sheet nor in shroud we wound him;
But he lay like a warrior taking his rest,
   With his martial cloak around him.

Few and short were the prayers we said,
   And we spoke not a word of sorrow;
But we steadfastly gazed on the face of the dead,
   And we bitterly thought of the morrow.

We thought, as we hollowed his narrow bed,
   And smoothed down his lonely pillow,
That the foe and the stranger would tread o'er his head,
   And we far away on the billow!

Lightly they'll talk of the spirit that's gone,
   And o'er his cold ashes upbraid him,
But little he'll reck, if they let him sleep on
   In the grave where a Briton has laid him.

But half of our heavy task was done,
   When the clock struck the hour for retiring;
And we heard the distant and random gun
   That the foe was sullenly firing.

Slowly and sadly we laid him down,
   From the field of his fame fresh and gory;
We carved not a line, and we raised not a stone—
   But we left him alone with his glory!—WOLFE.

### THE LITTLE DAISY.

Down in the country, not far from the roadside, stands a country house. In the front is a little garden, surrounded by painted palings. In the midst of the luxuriant green grass there grew a little daisy. The sun shone down as warmly upon her as on the beautiful ornamental flowers in the garden, and, therefore, she kept growing hour by hour. One morning she appeared with her little, dazzling, white leaves quite unfolded, like so many beams round the tiny yellow sun in the middle. She never thought that there was no one to see her here in the grass, and that she was a poor, despised flower,—no! she felt quite pleased, as she turned towards the warm sun, and looked up at it, and listened to the lark singing high above in the air.

The little daisy was as happy as if it had been a holiday. All the children were at school; and, while they were busy learning something, she sat on her little green stem, and she, too, learned from the warm sun, and from all that surrounded her, how infinite is the goodness of God. And she was delighted that the little lark should sing so plainly and so beautifully what she but inwardly felt.

And the daisy looked up with a sort of respect to the happy bird, who could warble and fly, yet without being afflicted that she herself could do neither.

"I can see, and I can hear," thought she; "the sun shines upon me, and the wind kisses me. Oh! how richly have I been gifted!"

Inside the palings stood a number of stiff, proud flowers.

The less perfume they possessed, the more they boasted. The peonies puffed themselves up, in order to be larger than the rose, but size is not everything. The tulips possessed the most gorgeous colours, and they knew this so well, that they stood as upright as a taper, in order to be admired the better. They took no notice of the little daisy outside; but she only looked the more at them, and thought, "How rich and how beautiful they are! The pretty bird will, of course, fly down and visit them! I am pleased that I stand near enough to contemplate their magnificence." And just as she was thinking so, the lark flew down, but not to the peonies and the tulips; no, but to the humble daisy in the grass. She was frightened out of mere joy, so that she knew not what to think.

The little bird hopped around her, singing, "Oh, how soft is the grass! And what a lovely little flower that is, with gold in its heart, and silver on its garment! for the yellow spot in the daisy looked like gold, and the little leaves around were as dazzlingly white as silver.

No one can tell how happy the daisy felt! The bird kissed her with his beak, and then soared back into the blue air above. It was a full quarter of an hour before the flower could recover from her emotion. Half ashamed, yet thrilling with delight, she cast a glance towards the flowers in the garden. They had seen the honour and the happiness that had been conferred upon her, and they must be aware how great was such a joy. But the tulips stood stiffer than ever: only their faces looked redder because they were vexed, while the peonies were no less annoyed. The poor little flower could see they were out of temper, and she was heartily sorry for it. At this moment a girl came into the garden with a large, sharp, shining knife in her hand, and went straight up to the tulips, and cut down one after another.

"Oh, dear!" sighed the little daisy; "this is shocking!"

The girl then carried the tulips away. The daisy rejoiced at being outside the garden, in the grass, and merely a poor little flower, and felt most thankful for her humble lot; and when the sun set, she folded up her leaves, and went to sleep, and dreamed the whole night long of the sun and of the little bird.

Next morning, when the flower once more gladly spread all her white leaves, like so many little arms stretching forth towards the air and the light, she recognised the bird's voice, but this time he sang mournfully—and well he might, for he had become a prisoner, and sat in a cage near an open window. He sang of the delights of flying about free and unfettered; he sang of the young, green corn, that he saw growing up in the fields, and of the pleasant journeys that birds on the wing are able to perform in the upper regions of the air. The poor bird was not in good spirits, for he was a prisoner in a cage.

The little daisy would gladly have helped him. But what could she do? It was a difficult matter to decide. She forgot how beautiful was all around, how warm the sunshine felt, and how white and pretty her leaves appeared. Alas! she could think of nothing but the captive bird, whom she was powerless to assist.

Just then, two little boys came out of the garden. One of them carried in his hand a large sharp knife, like the one the girl had used to cut the tulips. They went right up to the little daisy, who could not imagine what they wanted.

"We can cut out a nice tuft of grass here for the lark," said one of the boys, and began to cut a square piece round the daisy, so that she would stand in the centre of the plot.

"Pull up the flower!" said the other boy, while the daisy trembled with alarm; for to be plucked was the same as losing her life; and she wished to live, as she was to be taken with the piece of grass to the captive lark in his cage.

"No, let it be," said the other boy, "it looks so pretty." And so the flower was let alone, and taken into the lark's cage.

The poor bird was lamenting loudly over his lost freedom, and flapping his wings against the wires of the cage. The little daisy, not being able to speak, could not say a word of comfort, willingly as she would have done so. The whole morning was spent in this manner.

"Here is no water," said the captive lark; "they are all gone out and have forgotten to give me a drop to drink. My throat is parched and burning. I feel as if I had fire and ice within me, and the air is so heavy! Alas! I must die; and bid farewell to the warm sunshine, to the green grass, and to all the beautiful things in the world!" and he then drilled a hole with his beak in the cool patch of grass, in hopes of allaying his thirst.

He then happened to see the daisy, and nodded to her, and kissed her with his bill, saying, "You, too, will wither here, you poor little flower! yourself, and this little patch of green grass, is all that has been given me in exchange for the whole world that I enjoyed abroad! Each little blade of grass must serve me for a green tree; each of your white leaves must stand instead of a fragrant flower! Alas! you only tell me of all I have lost!"

"Would that I could comfort him!" thought the daisy; but she could not move a leaf. Yet, the perfume wafted from her leaves was much stronger than is usual with this flower; and the bird perceived as much, for, though he was pining with thirst, and tore up the green blades of grass in his anguish, yet he did not touch the flower.

It was now evening, and nobody had yet come to bring

the poor bird a drop of water. He spread out his pretty wings, and shook them convulsively; his song was mournful. His little head bent towards the flower, and the bird's heart broke with vain longing to quench his thirst. Neither could the flower fold up her leaves and go to sleep, as she did the night before, but sick and mournful she drooped towards the earth.

It was only on the following morning that the boys came, and when they found the bird dead, they shed many, many bitter tears, and buried him in a pretty grave, which they decked with flowers. The bird's lifeless form was laid in a smart, red box, because he was to be buried with regal honours. Poor bird! while he was living and singing they forgot him, and left him to suffer want in his cage,—now he was to be treated with state, and was mourned with many tears.

But the patch of grass with the daisy on it was thrown into the dust of the road. Nobody thought of the humble flower who had felt the most for the little bird, and who would so willingly have comforted him.—ANDERSEN'S TALES.

### THE BLIND MAN AND THE DEAF MAN.

A blind man and a deaf man once entered into partnership. The deaf man was to see for the blind man, and the blind man was to hear for the deaf man.

One day they both went to a nautch (musical and dancing entertainment) together. The deaf man said, "The dancing is very good, but the music is not worth listening to;" and the blind man said, "On the contrary, I think the music very good, but the dancing is not worth looking at."

After this they went together for a walk in the jungle, and there they found a washerman's donkey that had strayed away from its owner, and a great big jar (such as the washermen boil clothes in) which the donkey was carrying with him.

The deaf man said to the blind man, " Brother, here are a donkey, and a washerman's great big jar, with nobody to own them! let us take them with us, they may be useful to us some day." " Very well," said the blind man, " We will take them with us." So the blind man and the deaf man went on their way, taking the donkey and the great big jar with them. A little further on they came to an ant's nest, and the deaf man said to the blind man, " Here are a number of very fine black ants, much larger than any I ever saw before, let us take some of them home to show our friends." " Very well," answered the blind man, " We will take them as a present to our friends." So the deaf man took a silver snuff-box out of his pocket, and put four or five of the finest black ants into it; which done, they continued their journey.

But before they had gone very far a terrible storm came on. It thundered, and lightened, and rained, and blew with such fury that it seemed as if the whole heavens and earth were at war. " Oh, dear! oh, dear!" cried the deaf man, " How dreadful this lightning is; let us make haste and get to some place of shelter." " I do not see that it is dreadful at all," answered the blind man, " but the thunder is very terrible; we had better certainly seek some place of shelter."

Now, not far off was a lofty building, which looked exactly like a fine temple. The deaf man saw it, and he and the blind man resolved to spend the night there; and having reached the place, they went in and shut the door, taking the donkey and the great big jar with them. But this building, which they mistook for a temple, was in truth no temple at all, but the house of a very powerful Rakshas (demoniacal Ogre); and hardly had the blind man, the deaf man, and the donkey got inside, and fastened the door, than the Rakshas who had been out, returned home. To his surprise he found the door fastened, and heard people moving about inside his house. "Ho! ho!" cried he to himself, "Some men have got in here, have they! I will soon put an end to this." So he began to roar in a voice louder than the thunder, and he cried, "Let me into my home this minute, you wretches! let me in, let me in, I say," and to kick the door and batter it with his great fists. But though his voice was very powerful, his appearance was still more alarming, insomuch that the deaf man, who was peeping at him through a chink in the wall; felt so frightened that he did not know what to do. But the blind man was very brave, (because he could not see) and went up to the door, and called out, "Who are you? and what do you mean by coming battering at the door in this way, and at this time of night?"

"I am a Rakshas," answered the Rakshas angrily, "and this is my home, let me in this instant, or I will kill you." All this time the deaf man, who was watching the Rakshas, was shivering and shaking in a dreadful fright, but the blind man was very brave, (because he could not see) and he called out again, "Oh you are a Rakshas are you! well, if you are a Rakshas, I am Bakshas; and Bakshas is as good as Rakshas." "Bakshas," roared the Rakshas, "Bakshas! Bakshas! what nonsense is this? there is no such creature as a Bakshas!" "Go away," replied the blind man, "and do not dare to make any further disturbance, lest I punish you with a vengeance! for I know that I am Bakshas! and Bakshas is Rakshas's father." "My father?" answered the Rakshas. "Heavens and earth! Bakshas, and my father? I never heard such an extraordinary thing in my life. You my father, and in there? I never knew my father was called Bakshas?"

"Yes," replied the blind man; "go away instantly, I command you, for I am your father, Bakshas." "Very well,' answered the Rakshas (for he began to get puzzled and frightened) "but, if you are my father, let me first see your face." (For, he thought, "Perhaps they are deceiving me.") The blind man and the deaf man did not know what to do; but at last they opened the door—a very tiny chink—and poked the donkey's nose out. When the Rakshas saw it he thought to himself, "Bless me, what a terribly ugly face my father, Bakshas, has!" He then called out, "O, father Bakshas, you have a very big, fierce face! but people have sometimes very big heads and very little bodies. Pray let me see you, body as well as head, before I go away." Then the blind man and the deaf man rolled the great big jar with a thundering noise past the chink in the door, and the Rakshas, who was watching attentively, was very much surprised when he saw this great black thing rolling along the floor, and he thought, "In truth, my father Rakshas has a very big body, as well as a big head. He is big enough to eat me up altogether. I had better go away." But still he could not help being a little doubtful, so he cried, "O, Bakshas, father Bakshas! you have indeed got a very big head and a very big body; but do, before I go away, let me hear you scream" (for all Rakshas scream fearfully). Then the cunning deaf man (who was getting less frightened) pulled the silver snuff-box out of his pocket, and took the black ants out of it, and put one black ant in the donkey's right ear, and another black ant in the donkey's left ear, and another, and another. The ants pinched the poor donkey's ears dreadfully, and the donkey was so hurt and frightened, he began to bellow as loud as he could, "Eh augh! eh augh!" and at this terrible noise the Rakshas fled away in a great fright, saying, "Enough! enough! father Bakshas, the sound of your voice would make the most refractory obedient." And no sooner had he gone, than the deaf man took the ants out of the donkey's ears, and he and the blind man spent the rest of the night in peace and comfort.

Next morning the deaf man woke the blind man early, saying, "Awake, brother! awake! here we are indeed in luck! the whole floor is covered with heaps of gold, and silver, and precious stones!" And so it was; for the Rakshas owned a vast amount of treasure, and the whole house was full of it. "That is a good thing," said the blind man. "Show me where it is, and I will help you to collect it." So they collected as much treasure as possible, and made four great bundles of it. The blind man took one great bundle, the deaf man took another; and, putting the other two great bundles on the donkey, they started off to return home. But the Rakshas, whom they had frightened away the night before, had not gone very far off, and was waiting to see what his father, Bakshas, might look like by daylight. He saw the door of his house open, and watched attentively, when out walked—only a blind man, a deaf man, and a donkey, who were all three laden with large bundles of his treasure! The blind man carried one bundle, the deaf man carried another bundle, and two bundles were on the donkey.

The Rakshas was extremely angry, and immediately called six of his friends to help him kill the blind man, the deaf man, and the donkey, and recover the treasure.

The deaf man saw them coming (seven great Rakshas, with hair a yard long, and tusks like an elephant's), and was dreadfully frightened! but the blind man was very brave (because he could not see) and said, "Brother, why do you lag behind in that way?" "Oh!" answered the deaf man, "there are seven great Rakshas with tusks like an elephant's coming to kill us; what can we do?" "Let us hide the treasure in the bushes," said the blind man; "and do you lead me up to a tree: then I will climb up first, and you shall climb up afterwards, and so we shall be out of their way." The deaf man thought this good advice, so he pushed the donkey and the bundles of treasure into the bushes, and led the blind man to a high tree that grew close by; but he was a very cunning man, this deaf man, and instead of letting the blind man climb up first, and following him, he got up first, and let the blind man clamber after, so that he was further out of harm's way than his friend.

When the Rakshas arrived at the place, and saw them both perched out of reach in the tree, he said to his friends, "Let us get on each other's shoulders, we shall then be high enough to pull them down." So one Rakshas stooped down, and the second got on his shoulders, and the third on his, and the fourth on his, and the fifth on his, and the sixth on his, and the seventh and the last Rakshas (who had invited all the others) was just climbing up, when the deaf man (who was looking over the blind man's shoulder) got so frightened, that in his alarm he caught hold of his friend's arm, crying, "They are coming! they are coming!" The blind man was not in a very secure position, and was sitting at his ease, not knowing how close the Rakshas were. The consequence was, that when the deaf man gave him this unexpected push, he lost his balance, and tumbled down on to the neck of the seventh Rakshas, who was just then climbing up. The blind man had no idea where he was, but thought he had got on to the branch of some other tree; and, stretching out his hand for something to catch hold of, caught hold of the Rakshas' two great ears, and pinched them very hard in his surprise and fright. The Rakshas could not think what it was that had come tumbling down upon him: and the weight of the blind man upsetting his balance, down he also fell to the ground, knocking down in their turn the sixth, fifth, fourth, third, second, and first Rakshas, who all rolled one over another, and lay in a confused heap at the foot of the tree together. Meanwhile, the deaf man (who was safe up in the tree) answered, "Well done, brother! never fear! never fear! You are all right, only hold on tight. I am coming down to help you!" But he had not the least intention of leaving his place of safety. However, he continued to call out, "Never mind, brother! hold on as tight as you can. I am coming! I am coming!" and the more he called out, the harder the blind man pinched the Rakshas' ears, which he mistook for some kind of palm branches. The six other Rakshas, who had succeeded, after a good deal of kicking, in extricating themselves from their unpleasant position, thought they had had quite enough of helping their friend, and ran away as fast as they could; and the seventh, thinking from their going that the danger must be greater than he imagined, and being, moreover, very much afraid of the mysterious creature that sat on his shoulders, put his hands to the back of his ears, and pushed off the blind man: and then (without staying to see who or what he was) followed his six companions as fast as he could.

As soon as all the Rakshas were out of sight, the deaf man came down from the tree, and, picking up the blind man, embraced him, saying, "I could not have done better myself. You have frightened away all our enemies, but you see I came to help you as fast as possible." He then dragged the donkey and the bundles of treasure out of the bushes, gave the blind man one bundle to carry, took the second himself, and put the remaining two on the donkey, as before. But, when they had got nearly out of the jungle, the deaf man said to the blind man, "We are now close to the village; but if we take all this treasure home with us, we shall run great risk of being robbed. I think our best plan would be to divide it equally, then you shall take care of your half, and I will take care of mine, and each one can hide his share here in the jungle, or wherever pleases him best." "Very well," said the blind man, "do you divide what we have in the bundles into two equal portions, keeping one-half yourself, and giving me the other." But the cunning deaf man had no intention of giving up half of the treasure to the blind man, so he first took his own bundle of treasure and hid it in the bushes, and then he took the two bundles off the donkey and hid them in the bushes; and he took a good deal of treasure out of the blind man's bundle, which he also hid. Then, taking the small quantity that remained, he divided it into two equal portions, and, placing half before the blind man, and half in front of himself, said, "There, brother, is your share, to do what you please with." The blind man put out his hand, but when he felt what a very little heap of treasure it was, he got very angry, and cried, "This is not fair, you are deceiving me; you have kept almost all the treasure for yourself, and only given me a very little." "Oh, oh! how can you think so?" answered the deaf man: "but if you will not believe me, feel for yourself. See! my heap of treasure is no larger than yours." The blind man put out his hands again, to feel how much his friend had kept; but in front of the deaf man lay only a very small heap, no larger than what he had himself received. At this, he got very cross, and said, "Come, come, this will not do! You think you can cheat me in this way because I am blind; but I am not so stupid as all that. I carried a great bundle of treasure; you carried a great bundle of treasure; and there were two great bundles on the donkey. Do you mean to pretend that all that made no more treasure than these two little heaps? No, indeed, I know better than that!" "Nonsense!" answered the deaf man. "Nonsense or no nonsense," continued the other, "you are trying to deceive me, and I will not be defrauded by you." "No, I am not!" said the deaf man. "Yes, you are," said the blind man; and so they went on scolding, growling, contradicting, until the blind man got so enraged that he gave the deaf man a tremendous box on the ear. The blow was so violent, that it made the deaf man hear! The deaf man, very angry, gave his neighbour in return so hard a blow in the face, that it opened the blind man's eyes!

So the deaf man could hear as well as see! and the blind man could see as well as hear! This astonished them both so much, that they became good friends at once. The deaf man confessed that he had hidden the bulk of the treasure, which he thereupon dragged forth from its place of concealment, and, having divided it equally, they went home and enjoyed themselves.—FRERE's OLD DECCAN DAYS.


### A PSALM OF LIFE.

Tell me not, in mournful numbers,
    Life is but an empty dream!
For the soul is dead that slumbers,
    And things are not what they seem.

Life is real! life is earnest!
    And the grave is not its goal;
Dust thou art, to dust returnest,
    Was not spoken of the soul.

Not enjoyment, and not sorrow,
　　Is our destined end or way;
But to act, that each to-morrow
　　Find us farther than to-day.

Art is long, and time is fleeting,
　　And our hearts though stout and brave,
Still, like muffled drums, are beating
　　Funeral marches to the grave.

In the world's broad field of battle,
　　In the bivouac of life,
Be not like dumb, driven cattle!
　　Be a hero in the strife!

Trust no future, howe'er pleasant!
　　Let the dead past bury its dead!
Act—act in the living present!
　　Hearts within, and God o'erhead!

Lives of great men all remind us
　　We can make our lives sublime,
And, departing, leave behind us
　　Footprints on the sands of time;

Footprints, that perhaps another,
　　Sailing o'er life's solemn main,
A forlorn and shipwrecked brother,
　　Seeing, shall take heart again.

Let us, then, be up and doing,
　　With a heart for any fate;
Still achieving, still pursuing,
　　Learn to labour and to wait.—LONGFELLOW.

www.ingramcontent.com/pod-product-compliance
Lightning Source LLC
LaVergne TN
LVHW061214060426
835507LV00016B/1923